D0045801

In praise of *God Land*:

"*God Land* is a stubbornly hopeful book about how the places of faith we belong to might someday belong to us."
　　　　　—Kate Bowler, podcast host and author of *New York Times* bestseller
　　　　　　Everything Happens for a Reason (and other lies I've loved)

"Lyz Lenz's *God Land* is deeply critical and probing, but also generous and uncynical. Lenz writes with fury and tenderness, pursuing uncomfortable questions of faith, community, and self with unyielding tenacity. She writes as beautifully about ugliness and frustration as she does about love and grace. And the conclusions she reaches about herself, her religion, and her country are bracing in their thoughtful honesty."
　　　　　—Josh Gondelman, coauthor (with Joe Berkowitz) of *You Blew It*

"*God Land*, Lyz Lenz's much-anticipated debut book, is a marvel. . . . After laying bare all manner of losses of faith, both personal and community, Lenz journeys to a sense of hope, rooted in generosity, that is fully earned. *God Land* will expand your horizons on what this country offers and who inhabits it, and why we're better off journeying together, rather than apart."
　　　　　—Sarah Weinman, author of *The Real Lolita: The Kidnapping of*
　　　　　　Sally Horner and the Novel That Scandalized the World

"*God Land* is a remarkable work of reporting, memoir, and cultural criticism—a blazingly intelligent book exploring the ways that faith can both create and scatter communities in America. Lenz's beautiful prose—by turns brutal, lyrical, Biblical, and richly comic—propels the reader along with her on this journey through the churches and faith communities of the Midwest."
　　　　　—Ted Scheinman, author of *Camp Austen*

"*God Land* gives testimony to human resiliency amid personal and collective trauma. With keen journalistic insights and vulnerable storytelling, Lyz Lenz provides a clear-eyed account of loss and alienation within communities throughout middle America, but she also honors her and others' remarkable ability to pick up the pieces and to keep going when all seems lost."
　　　　　—Katelyn Beaty, author of *A Woman's Place*

"Lyz Lenz writes the story of so many of us—those who have been betrayed by American Christianity and yet are being reborn in the ashes of a new kind of faith. For those seeking to understand the divides of religion—including urban/rural, racial, and liberal/progressive—*God Land* serves as an intimate chance to listen to an insider account of why people are leaving the faith (and why some remain). Lenz is a funny, irreverent, and keen-eyed writer, who succeeds in converting us to both love and mourn the place of our country known as middle America."
　　　　　—D. L. Mayfield, activist and author of *Assimilate or Go Home:*
　　　　　　Notes from a Failed Missionary on Rediscovering Faith

GOD
LAND

A STORY OF FAITH, LOSS, AND
RENEWAL IN MIDDLE AMERICA

LYZ LENZ

INDIANA UNIVERSITY PRESS

This book is a publication of

Indiana University Press
Office of Scholarly Publishing
Herman B Wells Library 350
1320 East 10th Street
Bloomington, Indiana 47405 USA

iupress.indiana.edu

Manufactured in the United States of America

Cataloging information is available from the Library of Congress.

ISBN 978-0-253-04153-1 (hdbk.)
ISBN 978-0-253-04155-5 (web PDF)

1 2 3 4 5   24 23 22 21 20 19

CONTENTS

ACKNOWLEDGMENTS

W HENEVER A WOMAN DOES ANYTHING—WRITE A BOOK, create a life, have a career—the labor is often manifold and doesn't come with a break from laundry, homework, floor scrubbing, or cooking. During the course of writing this book, my whole life changed. I went from being married to being a single mom. But I still had kids. I still had dirty floors. Sometimes this was a blessing, often it was overwhelming as hell.

So many of my friends stepped in to help me with childcare, house cleaning, meal preparation, moving, furniture assembly, and so much more. They were the women of my community cheering me on. Offering me support, advice, book recommendations, sending me articles, giving me feedback, mailing me sassy socks, sending me kind texts and direct messages. Always with their loving and generous spirits, even when I was too overwhelmed to say "thank you."

They are my true church of the air—the community of women throughout the internet and in my town, without whom this book would not be. Without whom I would not be. Some of their names are Melanie Ostmo, Kristin Engle, Jeanne Towell, Yara Conway, Jessie Lowe, Megan Sova-Tower, Claire Zulkey, and all the witches.

I also want to thank my agent, Saba Sulaiman, who believed in my writing when no one else did. Ashley Runyon, who saw a book inside an internet article. And Ted Scheinman, an amazing and thoughtful editor, whose feedback, friendship, wisdom, and prompt responses to my pitches not only gave me a platform for my first thoughts on this subject, but also gave my words a home.

I also want to thank all the people who talked to me for this project, especially Mark Jackel-Juleen, who put me on the right course, and Evelyn Birkby, whose insight, generosity, and gift of time was foundational to my work.

Thanks to Pastor Ritva, who has never once asked me to work in a nursery.

My brother Zach is my best friend, and even though I still maintain he is the worst, he is also the best. His encouragement and terrible jokes have helped my words and my story find life. And all of my siblings, who taught me that we can all touch the same truth and walk away with different answers. And my parents, who raised me with love, God, and books and have always had my back even when I've sold them out on the page.

My friends Elon Green, Sarah Weinman, Nicole Cliffe, and Sarah Galo. You know what you did. Also, Marisa Seigel, Pam Colloff, Amy Sullivan, Kate Bowler, Deborah Jian Lee, Kathy Khang, Katelyn Beaty, Laura Turner, and Julie Rogers. And of course, Katie Bukowski, Anna Marsh, and Kate Johansen.

And of course to my children, Jude and Ellis, who are the most incredible human beings I've ever met.

GOD LAND

INTRODUCTION

IN FEBRUARY OF 2005, MY FIANCÉ AND I sped down Interstate 35 in his gold Mazda on our way to Iowa. Just across the border from Minnesota, a large sign read, "Iowa: Fields of Opportunity!" Half a mile later, another sign, this one handwritten on a piece of cardboard, read, "Acreage for sale!" I laughed. And then, a few minutes later, I was crying.

I didn't want to move. I wanted to stay in Minneapolis, a city where I felt I had real opportunities. Instead, I was getting married and moving to Cedar Rapids, Iowa, a city that at the time didn't have a freestanding Starbucks. Not that I like Starbucks, but in my mind it was a marker of civilization. Instead, what I had were bookstores and Targets that "proudly" brewed Starbucks coffee.

"Even Wisconsin has a Starbucks," I said as I looked out the window at the endless gray skies and the frozen dead fields full of nothing except snow and the remnants of a growing season that seemed so far away.

As we drove into Cedar Rapids, the place we would soon call home, Dave pointed out restaurants and stores. "Look, an Applebee's! You like hamburgers!"

"Look, a Famous Footwear! You like shoes!"

I nodded gamely. I wanted to be a team player. I wanted this to work. But I felt so lost in a city where I was never more than five minutes from an open field.

And he assured me we'd move back one day—for my career, once his was established. It's the kind of compromise that couples forge to make their mutual dreams and ambitions coexist—your turn, then my turn. The give and take of any functioning relationship. The foundation of a functional society—your turn, then my turn.

Dave and I were often trying to compromise. We couldn't have been more opposite. Him, quiet. Me, loud. Him, conservative. Me, two steps away from joining Greenpeace. But we'd make it work. Whatever divide, we would overcome it.

Eleven years later, Donald Trump was elected president. And just a year after that, I moved out and filed for divorce. We hadn't been able to make it work. The space between us was too big. Neither of us knew exactly when it happened. But it had come up on us slowly, like boiling a frog in water. Except the frog is wearing a MAGA hat. Or maybe that's not entirely honest. Maybe we had been so busy trying to make it work that we ignored the larger rifts—the fights we had over politics and religion. So determined to unite that we gaslit ourselves about reality.

From 2005 to 2017, the space between us grew and grew, stretching the limits of any compromise we were willing to make. It was a personal break that mirrored the national one. I had supported Hillary Clinton. He had voted for Donald Trump. And once we realized that, our marriage was so broken there was no fixing it.

Middle America is a dissonant space, pulled between the extremes of the coast. We have the reputation of being a moderating, milquetoast place, full of bland casseroles we call hot dish and passive aggressive assurances that we are fine. FINE. Or in the more elegant words of the Dar Williams song, "We don't like to make our passions other people's concerns." But to believe so fully in the bland passivity and unity of Middle America is to miss a more complex reality—contradictions, opposites, dissonance, that pulls, screams, and threatens to break this uniting middle space of our country. We ignore it at our peril.

Iowa was the third state to legalize gay marriage, but also continues to re-elect a bigoted congressman, Steve King. Places like Minneapolis, St. Louis, and Chicago are deeply diverse, while the senators and governors who oversee them are often deeply reactionary to immigration.

Because of this, Middle America resists representation. In our minds, no one can get us right. I've heard locals quibble over Marilynne Robinson's depictions of Iowa and Garrison Keillor's descriptions of Minnesota. Only Laura Ingalls is allowed to get it right, but that's because she lived through the Long Winter and earned it. We mock those journalists who fly in during presidential campaigns and write trend pieces on us.

Even if you are from here and you write about this place, there is often pushback and anger. "You don't know us and you can never know us," one angry commenter wrote in response to a story I had written about a small town in Iowa. I knew people from the town. I had spent years visiting the town, which was only a one-hour drive from my house. For the story, I'd spent months interviewing, visiting, and researching. I'd been fact-checked and I'd followed up with my sources.

This wasn't the first time I'd been told I had no right to talk about the Midwest and its specificities. And while I am not a perfect writer, and definitely not above reproach in my descriptions, it was clear that the complexities of place are resistant to a portrait rendered on the page. Midwestern historian Andrew R. L. Cayton writes, "Localism, this pride in family, town, and state, leaves little room for interest in a coherent regional identity. In general, Midwesterners want to be left alone in worlds of their own making."[1]

And this resistance to description lends itself to an almost universality. Phil Christman, a writer and teacher at Michigan State University, explains in his essay "On Being Midwestern: The Burden of Normality" that Midwesterners "think of ourselves as basic Americans, with no further qualification. 'The West, South, and East all have clear stories,' as Katy Rossing puts it. But in the Midwest, we don't. We're free. And that is our story."[2]

This is the reason Iowa is first in the nation for caucuses. The reason politicians proudly declare that they've shaken hands with "folks" in the Midwest. Because in our resistance to representation, we are believed to be so basically normal. So overwhelmingly American. That's what you are told when you ask a person in Middle America to describe it here—once you get past the clichés of good schools and "it's a good place to live," Middle America's most notable quality is its presumed normality.

Christman continues:

> Small wonder, then, that Midwestern cities, institutions, and people show up again and again in the twentieth-century effort to determine what, in America, is normal. George Gallup was born in Iowa, began his career in Des Moines at Drake University, and worked for a time at Northwestern; Alfred Kinsey scandalized the country from—of all places—Bloomington, Indiana. Robert and Helen Lynd, setting out in the 1920s to study the "interwoven trends that are the life of a small American city," did not even feel the need to defend the assumption that the chosen city "should, if possible, be in that common-denominator of America, the Middle West." They chose Muncie, Indiana, and called it Middletown. We cannot be surprised that the filmgoers of Peoria became proverbial, or that newscasters are still coached to sound like they're from Kansas.[3]

Of course, like a person in the Midwest, I am going to quibble with all of this and say it isn't entirely accurate. There is a lot of America not represented in the Midwest and there is, of course, a lot of disagreement about what exactly is the Midwest.

My choice to focus on the Midwest was motivated by a desire to interrogate this idea of "normality." Demographically and geographically, of course, the Midwest isn't normal. But this is the place we've made the standard-bearer for what is American and by extension what are American values. What is happening to churches in Middle America is not just about church or faith; it's a fight over American values.

I'm in no way trying to legitimize the efforts to glorify the Midwest as what America "ought" to be. Efforts like that are deeply racist and sexist and level the complex nuance of this large country. I live here. Middle America has become my home. I raise my children here. I love this wild and weird prairie—a landscape that has given to me just as much as I have given to it. But, as I hope becomes apparent throughout this book, I believe in the voices and experiences that come from outside of this region too. This book contains multitudes, but doesn't contain them all. This book is only once piece of a larger cultural conversation that I hope continues.

Practically, I define the Midwest the same way our government does: Iowa, Minnesota, Michigan, Indiana, Wisconsin, North Dakota, South Dakota, Illinois, Nebraska, Kansas, Ohio, and Missouri. These states comprise 21 percent of the total population of the United States. Of course, I have my peccadillos. I think that North Dakota, South Dakota, Nebraska, and Kansas are better defined as Great Plains states. And any place that doesn't have a defined lexicon of "hot dish" (I'm looking at you, Missouri) doesn't seem to be very Midwestern. But this is the definition that stands. And every place as big as America will have its factions and divisions.

While writing this book, I made the conscious decision to call this place "Middle America." I did this because it encapsulates the dominant mythology of the area, one that asserts this geographical space as a midpoint or bridge between the divided Americas of East and West, North and South.

I also did this in an effort to challenge the reader's conceptions of this place. Some representations, of course, will be familiar. Some will be different. But in the end, this story is my story, and the story of the land, of a place, of a people entirely other than me. The line between the stories is often murky. Sometimes it's hard to know where I end and where the rest of this place begins.

But that's why I wanted to write this, because the stakes of faith here are so personal. The divide in America is a divide that was replicated in my own marriage and my own faith life. It's a divide I have seen and felt in my communities: at my children's schools, in my family, at my gyms, and in my coffee shops. I wanted to know why my church failed. But I also wanted to know why churches across America were failing. And after the 2016 election, I wanted to know how and why the things I had always believed about my home—the neighborliness, the community—had all seemed to fail me too. This book is an attempt to understand these wounds, to grieve these losses, and if not to find a way out, then a way forward, through this mess we call America. A mess that's not external from us, but deeply ingrained in who we are as people.

There are other people's stories in here, and most often I have changed their names. I did that because many of the conversations we had were personal and happened even before the research for the book began. Other people wanted their privacy respected, and I hope I have done that. Just a few, like researchers and Evelyn Birkby, retain their own names. Many of the people in this book are friends and family, or became that through the writing. Sometimes I changed identifying information. But the truth of what they've said and their experiences remain.

Through their stories and mine, this book is an attempt to sit in the brokenness of our nation and our lives and seek to find redemption. I don't believe in bridges anymore. I don't even believe in fixing all broken things. Instead, what I believe is that we need to stare deep into the darkness of loss and to see the divine. When I began writing this book, it was because I wanted to understand this place and the losses it contains. But as I continued to write, I realized I needed to understand myself. And the two are not so significantly different.

1

DANGEROUS SPECULATION

W HEN I WONDER ABOUT WHERE THE CRACKS IN everything began, I go back to Stonebridge. Stonebridge was a church that my husband and I and six other friends tried to start in Marion, Iowa, in 2010. We were all frustrated with what we saw as faith in America. We were frustrated with faith in our town. And in the beginning, we were united in our grievances. In our estimation, the churches did little for the town. They had loud brassy bands and hip pastors, but no substance. There was no community. And everyone always looked the same. There had to be another way, and so we decided to make something for ourselves.

It's a very colonizing impulse to look at something—a land, a city, a culture—and instead of seeing what is there, see a barren landscape that needs your new ideas. It's an American impulse to see a problem and think you can solve it with a little hard work and some bootstraps. It's a deeply human impulse to look all around you and see a problem but never consider that you might be the actual problem. If we had, for a moment, pondered the logic of any one of our impulses, everything might have turned out differently. But we didn't. And so, we got into a mess.

The problem we saw that we wanted to solve was this: In our state there were anemic rural churches that lacked vibrancy. And vibrant city churches that lacked depth. We would change all of that. We'd build something small but robust. Something holy and relevant. Something meaningful and practical. Reading over our notes from those meetings feels a lot like asking a twenty-year-old man what he wants in a woman and hearing him say, "I want her to be outgoing, but also likes a night in. I want someone who likes to have fun, but will also cook a three-course meal. A lover and a mother. A simple woman, who has class and taste. Who loves to save money, but does all the shopping." In sum, we didn't know what the hell we wanted. But we thought we did. And at least we knew we didn't want any of the other places we'd been to.

Since moving to Cedar Rapids in 2005, Dave and I had attended almost twenty churches. One church we went to never invited us into a Bible study. When I asked a pastor or a Sunday school teacher about Wednesday night Bible studies, I was always told to ask someone else, who told me to ask someone else. This went on for five months, until one Sunday the pastor preached a sermon about the importance of small groups and said from the pulpit that all we had to do was ask to be invited. We never went back.

Or there was the church we visited in 2006 that sent three teams of elders to prayer walk around our townhouse. I sent them packing after I opened the door and asked them what they were doing. "Can we speak to your mom?" asked one of the older gentlemen in a suit and a tie.

"I am the mom," I said and slammed the door shut. They left a flyer under the door and walked around our townhouse praying once more, for good measure.

There was the church we visited in 2005, where we heard several sermons about not "jumping ship" when your "church goes bad." The "bad" was vague and never specified. Needless to say, we did not go back there either.

After three years of searching, Dave and I finally ended up at an Evangelical Free Church. It was there we met the couples we started Stonebridge with and got involved with the youth group. But even then, that church wasn't an easy fit for us. Or, I should be clear, it wasn't an easy fit for me. The church was a lot like the Evangelical churches Dave and I had attended as kids—raucous music, a pastor who gave sermons that often included video clips and pop-culture references. There was no liturgy, there were no organs, and most of the people who attended seemed to be our age. Few people drank, no one smoked, and they all loved to discuss the book of Revelation after one too many Mountain Dews at a church party.

While I loved the people there, I didn't like the church's theology. The church was and is very conservative; their theology was that of the Evangelical Free Church of America, which doesn't affirm women or gay people as pastors or elders. Here strict gender roles were enforced and even seen as freeing. Everybody was white.

As someone who doesn't like to wear bras on principle, I frequently found myself chafing against the strict orthodox interpretation of the Bible and the long lectures I was often given by male members of the church about how, if I believed women could be pastors, I was questioning the inerrancy of the Bible.

But in those early days of my marriage and my adult life, I thought that these problems were minor squabbles. Something to be hashed out over late nights playing board games and drinking wine, or wine for me, Fresca for the rest of them. It was a privilege, born of my childhood raised in a white Evangelical homeschool subculture in Texas. Until I went to high school at a public school, everyone I knew believed in a literal six-day creation by the hand and voice of God. Everyone believed that being gay was a sin. I was used to being the outsider—the lone voice of dissent. I was comfortable with this role because I wasn't threatened by it. Not yet, anyway. I wasn't gay. I wasn't a person of color. I was a woman, but the gentle grasp of patriarchy hadn't yet threatened to strangle me, because I hadn't yet tried to get free. Or perhaps I had, but I was so used to a religion that told me I was wrong and objectionable, it never occurred to me there could be another way.

Faith was also so much more to me than a God I occasionally sang songs to in church or prayed to over meals. Faith had provided the entire fabric of my life. It was the cytoplasm in which I existed—the amniotic fluid that sustained my relationships with my husband and my family. My mother read the Bible to us in the mornings, and my father read it to us before I went to sleep at night. I could not conceive of myself outside of religion.

I often thought about telling Dave or my parents that I didn't believe in God. That I no longer wanted to go to church. But how could I forsake the inheritance of my childhood? Even now, that deep-soul thump of God and eternal judgement still rises in me when I hear "I'll Fly Away" or "The Old Rugged Cross."

Because I could not imagine life outside the womb of my faith, I struggled inside its limitations. I thought there would always be room for me. But the reality was, there was only room for me if I made myself smaller and smaller and smaller, until I disappeared. Or else I'd be pushed out into a bright new horrible, beautiful world, where I would gasp and scream and try to breathe, for once, on my own.

But in those early days, I kicked around, trying to make my place, approaching my disagreements head on. During a membership class at our Evangelical church, the one we'd later leave, I eagerly debated the head pastor, Travis, over whether the Bible supported female ordination. My husband, who agreed with the church's stances, sat stony-faced as I recited the arguments I'd learned from my Lutheran friends and from reading books such as *Ten Lies the Church Tells Women*. The pastor gamely debated me, but stood strong. "I agree the topic needs more investigation," was all he would allow. And I took it, that proffered breadcrumb, as a promise to journey together—to listen to one another. I took it as a sign of respect. And that's all I needed. I didn't need to be right, I just needed to be treated like someone smart, someone with something to offer besides filling a nursery volunteer spot on Sunday mornings. I needed to be treated like a person.

The promised investigation never came. That offer was just a way of putting me off, shutting me up. A year later, when I asked if we could have a Bible study that opened up the topic, I wasn't shut down, I was just ignored. I asked the question of the pastor and he smiled and said, "I'll think about it." Nothing else. And every time I brought it up, that's what I was told. "I'll think about it."

Death by a thousand maybes.

It's a passive-aggressive technique—a denial by silence. There is nothing to fight against. Just resolute lips and an unfocused gaze that refuses to see you, your desperation, humanity, and longing. I'm used to that look. I get it a lot. Or at least, I used to.

I've spent my whole life in conservative Evangelical churches. Born the second of eight kids and raised in Texas, I spent my spiritual childhood hearing hour-long sermons in humid, brick churches filled with the Holy Spirit and hymns and pastors who sweat through their shirtsleeves proclaiming the second coming of the Lord.

In Sunday school, we looked for signs and revelations of the impending apocalypse: the tentative peace recently brokered in the Middle East, the talk of rebuilding the temple in Jerusalem, the war on religion we were told that Janet Reno was perpetuating with the attacks on Ruby Ridge and Waco. I went to sleep afraid I'd wake up to find my whole family raptured. When I went to the toilet, I prayed to Jesus not to call me up to heaven right then and there with my pants pulled down.

At home, my father taught us that numerology showed Hillary Rodham Clinton's name worked out to 666. My mother made us read *The Hiding Place*, and we talked about what we'd do in the End Times when we were persecuted for our faith.

I read Frank Peretti's books, hiding under the covers, dreaming about the thin veil between the spiritual world and the one where I bit my nails and prayed for Jesus to make me good. I was no good in the churches of my childhood—I was too loud, too demanding, I looked too much like a boy, I asked too many questions.

By the time I was eighteen years old, I'd been in small churches where pastors slept with congregants and in megachurches where youth pastors slept with teens. I'd seen gay women kicked out of the congregations they loved because they wouldn't apologize for who God created them to be. I'd seen my friend, pregnant at sixteen, asked to stop singing with the worship team, while the boy who was the father still led prayers on Wednesday nights. By the time I finally went to college, I had given up. For four years, I never went to chapel. I still believed in God, but I didn't believe in church.

After I graduated and married Dave, who'd been raised in the soft evangelicalism of the upper-middle-class, white, Midwestern suburbs, I was determined that we would find a new church together; one that fit both of us.

We moved to Cedar Rapids, Iowa, for his job, and the first thing he did was make a list of all the churches he wanted to visit, without my input. In hindsight, this wasn't a good sign. But it's also how he put together our budget, planned vacations, and bought cars. I had a choice—and that choice was to choose from the options on his spreadsheet. And when you are young and in love and used to the patriarchy as a modus operandi, well, you put up with a lot of things without thinking.

Dave and I worked through the list in alphabetical order until we finally settled into the Evangelical Free Church. We weren't looking for perfection, we just wanted a home. Or, more accurately, I wanted a home. I wanted a place that would accept all of me. Where I wouldn't be forced to hide my questions and my doubts, swallow my fears and outrage, and get along. Perhaps that's why, when Pastor Travis told me we'd talk about it later or that he was thinking about my idea of the Bible study examining the woman's role in the church, I took him at his word.

Compliance is easier than questioning. The appearance of unity is easier than the messy actualities. And I think part of me always understood that if I pushed too hard, I would be cast out of everything I knew. That I'd lose everything. So, I smiled during sermons I hated. I kept silent during Bible studies where people spoke of dinosaurs and humans roaming the earth together before Noah's flood.

Dave and I put everything into that church. We volunteered with the youth on Wednesday nights, I helped with the coffee every Sunday and in the nursery, and we went on a trip to Israel and on a mission trip to El Salvador. On that mission trip, everything fell apart. It fell apart because I asked to lead the prayer during devotionals one morning. Steven, the pastor leading the group, had frowned and told me that wasn't my place. I was furious. I had a specific story I wanted to share. One of our local hosts, who was a woman and a pastor, had taken me with her on her visits to the sick people in the village. I'd used my Spanish-English dictionary to talk to a man about how my sisters had been hit by a car, just like he had. How one of my sisters also had a hard time walking. It was a small moment of connection that I wanted to tell everyone about, and I wanted to pray for him.

But Steven was upset because I had been with a female pastor, and he didn't think it was my place to be leading devotions in our majority male group. Steven's approach even angered Dave. When I had told Steven that nothing in the Bible prevented me from talking out loud in a small group, he replied by saying, "It's there in the Scripture, right here where you are told to submit."

When Dave and I returned from the trip, we met with Pastor Travis and voiced our concerns. We had heard that other people had similar concerns with this same pastor, and I said as much.

"What? Who?" Travis said.

"You know who," I said. "They told me they told you."

"No one told me anything," he said.

My husband spoke up. "We know people have talked to you about how this man treats people."

Pastor Travis bowed his head and folded his hands for a moment. When he looked up, he met my husband's eyes and said, "You are right. I don't know why I lied and I apologize to you."

"Apologize to me," I said. "You lied to me, not to him."

"I did apologize to you when I apologized to your husband," Pastor Travis replied, looking not at me but at Dave. We had been going to that church for five years together and here I was, not even worthy of an apology.

I had trusted Pastor Travis. I had believed that, even though we disagreed, he saw me as a human—smart, worthy of time and consideration. But in that moment, with his resolute lips and gaze focused somewhere over my head, I saw that I wasn't a whole person to him. I wasn't even worthy of my own apology. Whatever story I had told myself about mutual respect turned out to be just a lie. That offer to "journey together" was just a coded way of saying, "You'll eventually grow up and agree with me." It wasn't the last time I heard that phrase.

Perhaps during his daily devotionals he had prayed for me to realize "the truth." Or more likely, he never thought about me at all in that church of eight hundred people. What did he even care for my theological disagreements? My hopes for honest and open discussion? After all, I'd shown up every Sunday for five years, volunteered with the children, made dishes for the potlucks. He'd had the compliance of my body in the service of his theology. What did he care for my mind and my thoughts?

So, Dave and I left.

Pastor Travis and Steven did try to reach out with apologies for the misunderstandings, but I refused to speak to them. There was no misunderstanding. I thought I was a smart person, fully capable of studying the Bible and engaging with spirituality on my own, and they disagreed. When someone denies the very core of who you are, it's hard to dialogue.

That's why we wanted to start a church. We got together with our friends, other castoffs from this same church, who had been alienated by Travis, and started planning. The group was four couples: me and Dave, Adam and Gina, Jim and Susan, Mattie and Tyler. It would be different, we vowed. We'd be small like a family. We'd help our community. We'd be open to other people and other voices. We'd be so different.

In *Transcendental Wild Oats*, a biting satire of her father's failed utopia, Fruitlands, Louise May Alcott notes: "To live for one's principles, at all costs, is a dangerous speculation; and the failure of an ideal, no matter how humane and noble, is harder for the world to forgive and forget than bank robbery or the grand swindles of corrupt politicians."[1]

It's a self-serving passage, delivered through the thoughts of Abel, a selfish man, who is in part bemoaning the fact that no one appreciates his genius. But in that paragraph, I hear a moment of humanity, where grace is offered by a daughter, even after her father's selfish actions had thrust her and her family into poverty one too many times. It is easy to spin dreams, harder to weave them into something practical.

I used to read that story and think of my parents, who homeschooled their children in the early 1980s and 1990s, when it was still marginally illegal. I think of my mother, who was fond of trying to get us to join cultish groups of fundamentalists, who spun their own yarn and made their own clothes. I think of my father, who always said "No."

But now that passage was about me. I had a dream: a church where Dave and I would both fit. And we began to make that a reality when I was just a couple weeks pregnant with our first child.

It was my turn to build a utopia. And it was my turn to fail.

Our church was dangerous speculation, an attempt to live an ideal. But in the end it's clear that we'd never agreed on what those ideals were. It's not that I didn't say anything. I remember all too clearly, sitting on the floor of Jim and Susan's house, saying, "I want us to affirm women as pastors. I want gay people to be welcome." I am trying to remember how they responded, but all I hear is silence. There was no response—just resolute lips and an unfocused look over my head. I knew the signs, but I didn't see them. We were friends after all. I trusted them.

I think back now, to all those late nights in Jim and Susan's house. The little oak shelves cluttered with pictures of their family, dried flowers, and small wooden figures of mothers and churches. We ate taco pizza together and played *Rock Band*. We sang worship songs to CDs with backing tracks. Our wobbly voices soft and hesitant, our Bibles always open.

Six months pregnant, I sat on the floor and argued that women had to be able to be pastors and had to at least be able to be elders. I know I fought to codify my wishes in our rules because Dave asked me to stop pushing for the issue one night as we drove home from a meeting.

"It's just, I've seen too many people say one thing and do another," I said. "I want to know that it's in the rules."

"Don't you trust us?" he asked.

And I did. That's the tragedy. I did trust them. Jim and Susan had been dear friends to us when Dave's father died. The other couple, Adam and Gina, were there when my sisters had been in a devastating car accident. The third couple, Mattie and Tyler, were newer friends, but already so dear. Their daughter was just a few months older than the baby inside me. The two girls would grow up best friends—fierce protectors of one another. Mattie would be there when I eventually ended my marriage and moved out. She spent too much money on Christmas decorations for my new house. "The kids need to know it's Christmas everywhere," she said when I protested.

But that would be seven years later. Now, I trusted all of them. I felt like I didn't have a choice. I had put myself in this dangerous speculation. I was working full time and would soon have a baby. It was easier to settle into the silence.

I want to be clear about this failure. This book is full of dangerous speculation and failure. This book is full of empty churches and broken hearts. It's a story of boarded-up stores and fierce and angry voices. It's the story of abuse of power and broken covenants. It's about faith, hope, and loss in America's heartland.

So, while it might be tempting to attribute these failures to "the imperfect nature of humanity," nothing can be further from the truth.

To excuse failure on man's imperfections—or in religious-speak, "sin nature"—is a careless kind of nihilism that gives an easy pass to the baser nature of religious leaders as merely being "imperfect" and these kinds of failures as unavoidable.

There are so many churches that remain strong, while being awful to women or providing safe havens for the power hungry. And there are so many good places that close despite being a home for the hungry, the lost, and the hurting. To brush off problems with churches as the problems of the inherently flawed nature of people is to miss the bigger picture: that life and faith can function together in a place where all are welcome and respected.

But that wasn't our church.

From the beginning, our pastor, Adam, repeatedly harangued other members about their commitment to the cause. When my daughter was six weeks old, I forgot to update the church's website. Adam sent me multiple emails accusing me of not having faith in our church and questioning my belief in God. Adam and Jim also excluded Mattie and Tyler from many church meetings because both had been previously divorced and therefore weren't "worthy" of leadership positions. Yet, when a married man who served as our worship leader later confessed to logging onto Match.com and dating other women, Adam and Jim argued that we should consider keeping him on in the role. I was outraged and refused to agree. I didn't even want to allow him to stand in front of our congregation and offer himself up like a martyr. I argued that this man's actions meant that he could no longer stand in front of us as a leader.

"You are so angry," Adam told me.

"I am," I said. "I didn't want our church to become a haven for abusers and here we are."

I won that fight. But the juxtaposition between that man and Mattie and Tyler was glaring. Mattie and Tyler weren't even involved in the conversation. I was later told it was because they weren't eligible to be elders.

As our church grew, Adam's behavior intensified. People approached me to tell me he'd accused them of not having a saving faith. Which in churchy lingo just means they think they are going to heaven but they aren't because they don't act holy enough. A couple desperately in need of counseling had been rebuffed and blown off. I was pregnant with my second child and working full time, and Adam accused me of not doing enough to support the women's ministry.

I told Dave that Adam was out of control. I forwarded every email and every complaint to Jim and Dave. Nothing happened. And I began to be shouldered out of conversations. Meetings happened and I didn't go because I had babies who were sick or tired, or I was sick or tired. But I began to wonder if that wasn't an excuse.

None of my beliefs had ever been codified into the rules. Adam just kept telling me we'd follow Scripture, but what that meant was unclear to me. Finally, nearly four years in, Adam came up with something that was so weird no one could ignore it. He had a plan to take over a local Methodist church. He laid it out for us one night at a meeting. He'd already spoken to the church and thought we could use their building for a Sunday night Bible study. The plan was, we'd just tell them we wanted to rent the space. But really we'd grow and grow and slowly and surreptitiously force them out. The congregation was aging, Adam reasoned, as if a planned coup of another church was perfectly normal. We were doing them a favor. Really, this was God's will.

The first thing I could think of to say was, "But you don't even like Methodists."

Adam glared at me.

"The denomination owns their building. Also, we have a lease on ours. This is crazy."

No one else said anything.

"I am disappointed in your lack of faith," Adam said.

This time I did laugh. "No amount of faith is gonna justify a coup d'etat on aging Methodists."

"I'm not a woman, so pardon me if I'm not quite as emotional about this, but maybe we need some time to think," Jim said.

I felt my body tense and I looked around the room. The walls we had painted. The chairs we'd cobbled together from Craigslist ads. The coffee bar that I carefully maintained, supplied, and decorated. The sounds of our kids' voices echoed from the back room. The table still had the cleaned dishes from the picnic. Those were the parts of this I understood. The things I had wanted.

But signing up to take over some Methodists was some next-level crazy. And apparently, because I was saying so in a group full of people, I was now an emotional woman. I waited for my husband to intervene. But he didn't. And that night, when I told Dave he should have supported me, we fought.

"You are not even an elder, Lyz," Dave said.

The baby started crying in the other room. And I started crying too. I was so tired. Tired from having two small children. Tired of not being seen as a human.

"I won't stay silent anymore," I said.

I called another meeting to discuss the issue. And another. I kept forcing the issue. I wanted everyone to agree that we would not be mean to Methodists. Getting that kind of buy-in was harder than you would think. We had three meetings over the course of three weeks and in the end Adam quit. Without the financial contribution from his family we could no longer pay the lease and we closed down the church.

We'd tried to unite. We'd tried to come together. But we failed.

We sold what we could. I gave away the excess tea and coffee to a women's shelter and then threw the rest in the trash. All the pieces of that church are in the trash: broken folding chairs, the package of neon-pink shot glasses I bought when we didn't have communion cups, the thrift-store plate I bought and covered in chalkboard paint to advertise the weekly coffee flavor (French vanilla! Hazelnut!). There were also two boxes of *Daily Bread*s, those little paper devotionals that populate the literature tables in Protestant churches. At our church, no one ever took them except my three-year-old daughter, who would scribble on every page. Sunday school coloring sheets with Moses and the burning bush, buckets of broken crayons, a single mitten, someone's dirty sock—I carried them out to the dumpster like so many offerings of failure. I even threw away a small New Testament and a pair of cheap silver earrings; I didn't know what else to do with them.

* * *

Across the heartland, churches are dying. Some, like mine, are bright bursts that ignite then die—leaving ash. Others die more slowly—a stubborn refusal to quit despite the loss of their communities, the loss of business, the loss of homes and jobs. All of them are utopias in the dreams of their members. All of them a dangerous speculation.

The loss of a church represents more than just a failure of a religious space. It represents the loss of social continuity and coherence. In Middle America, Christianity is so deeply woven into the very fabric of our society that even the biggest cities often don't have school activities on Wednesday nights, and many local bars and restaurants are closed on Sunday. To lose a church for whatever reason means losing an institution that offered narrative cohesion to your life and your concept of self. Whether you are a farmer in Wisconsin losing the Lutheran church that's been in the town for 150 years, or like me, a mom in a city losing the church she helped to start, the loss of a center of faith marks the loss of an ideal.

Our church failed for so many reasons: some personal, some political, and some just bat-shit insane. Yet, while our church and its problems were unique, our closure was not unique. All across Middle America, churches are shutting their doors. According to the Association of Religious Data Archives, between 1990 and 2010, Iowa lost more than five hundred congregations.[2] Supporting this data is an NPR analysis of a study from Georgetown University's Center for Applied Research in the Apostolate, which estimates that 10 percent of Catholic parishes have closed in the Midwest.[3]

The loss of these community centers—these spiritual homes—is changing the very landscape of the Midwest and the very fabric of our lives— interpersonally, politically, and socially.

The institutions that once formed the backbone of life in Middle America are crumbling. The Plymouth County Historical Museum, which is housed in the old La Mars High School, has a whole floor dedicated to the remnants of rural churches. Rows of drab old organs are huddled together on the yellowing linoleum. One room holds stained-glass windows, pulpits, and murals retrieved from the small white churches now atrophying in cornfields.

This loss is due, in part, to the continuing move from rural to urban life. Less than 2 percent of Americans are farmers. With the increased mechanization and corporatization of farms, neighbors become more far-flung. The cheap cost of gas means that people can more easily commute to work in the city and find their way back home. As the distance between neighbors grows, so too does the social space that separates them.

But there are other demographic trends at work too. Fewer people are attending churches. The *Des Moines Register* reported the results of a recent Pew study that found, "on average, about 54 percent of Iowans in 2010 attended a religious service or believed in a religion's ideas. That's about the same as in 1952 but down 8 percentage points from 1971."[4]

They are small shifts, but in an area of the country that has seen the atrophy of schools, jobs, and now faith, the impact is deeply felt.

* * *

In 1998 Mark Brodin saw his church in Delafield Township in Wisconsin close for reasons he was at a loss to explain. He made the documentary *Delafield* as both a memorial to the importance of churches in rural communities and as a way to understand the loss. His documentary focuses on the demographic shifts that Delafield faced. Once a farming community, it has seen the loss of agricultural jobs and rural out-migration. The population is aging and the people who stay have to travel farther for work. No young people came to church. The pastor in the documentary leaves a spot in the service for a children's sermon, but rarely does she get the chance to give one.

But this isn't just a rural problem. My own church, located in the middle of a city in Iowa, struggled to find and keep people in the pews. In Brodin's documentary, the aging congregants attribute the loss of a church-going population to a change in values. One woman in Brodin's documentary shouts with uncharacteristic Midwestern anger, "What does it mean to let the heartland go down the tube?" Although filmed in 1998, it felt just as real watching the documentary in 2018, two years after an election that revealed the deep, unbridgeable divide that had ripped America, not apart, but into many little pieces. And it's a sentiment I heard from the people in my own church as we closed our doors: *People just don't have good values anymore. Our heartland is going down the tubes.* It's a lament I've heard repeated over and over during the past two years of research as I've visited churches in Indiana, Minnesota, Wisconsin, and South Dakota and as I've emailed with pastors and spoken on the phone with congregants who have left never to return. I even heard this when I drank coffee at a Humanists meeting and had dinner at a Satanist potluck. I've thought this about others, as I've heard them justify policies and faith practices I don't agree with: "They just don't have good values." And I've heard that criticism leveled at me, when I've asked questions or disagreed with the people I've come to love as my neighbors and family.

This idea of values is not static. In her book *Those Who Work, Those Who Don't: Poverty, Morality, and Family in Rural America*, Jennifer Sherman[5] argues that this sense of morality is in flux. It's influenced, yes, by a Christian ethic, but also by the shifting ideals of ruralism, work ethic, and poverty in America. For example, one man I met was held as a paragon of virtue in his rural Illinois community. Yet, one of his biggest achievements, one that was touted to me by his own pastor, was his ability to build his home on his property in a way that allowed him to evade property taxes. Another minister, who has worked his whole life to protect and serve immigrants, told me that he proudly voted for Donald Trump because he thought Trump was God's chosen leader. In another chapter, I heard a pastor extol the virtues of carrying a gun while preaching, so he could shoot and kill anyone who walked in trying to do the same to him and his congregation.

Clearly, this isn't giving unto Caesar what is Caesar's, loving thy neighbor, or turning the other cheek. There is some other morality at play here, an idea of a civil religion deeply connected with Christianity but also influenced by capitalism, regionalism, and politics.

2

THE HEART OF THE HEARTLAND

BLUFF ROAD ROLLS OUT BEFORE ME—UP AND DOWN through farmland seeded with corn, soy, and low tin buildings. The landscape is broken only by the bare claws of chinquapin oak, and brushy pine. The ground rises and falls with undulations created by ancient winds. I'm told to just drive until I see it—the pioneer church.

I'm skeptical. My phone doesn't work out here and it's February. Although it's been unseasonably warm—in the 50s and 60s—I'm reminded of when I got my car stuck once before, on an icy country road in search of a pioneer church. That was almost a year ago, and then, as now, I was lost. Then when my wheels spun out on the ice, I panicked. I couldn't remember the last time I'd seen a house. So, I gathered sticks and put them under the wheels of my Mazda for traction. I put the car into drive then reverse, drive then reverse, rocking the car back and forth, spinning the wheels, and praying that I made it home in time to pick up my kids. It took forty minutes, but I finally got out. The damage was only a slight tear to the undercarriage of my car and the anxiety sweats I'd had while imagining myself dead in a field. I'd been only an hour away from my house then, but it felt so much farther on those gray roads that slump through the empty scabs of cold farmland.

Sometimes on these trips I believe I'm being swallowed by the earth—trees stretch their wooden phalanges over the roads, hills rise up and recede. Nature seems constantly on the verge of reclaiming what's hers. It makes going out again to find another pioneer church an act of faith. This time I ask for help, and the woman at the Sidney Drug Store tells me to turn off of Highway 2, go down Bluff Road and I'll see it.

Eventually, I do.

The church is right across the road from a split-level home, aging in tandem with the church. I pull into the driveway to ask permission to explore the church, and a dog comes out to greet me. I'm afraid I'll get bitten. I'm afraid I'll get yelled at. But I'm even more afraid of getting shot if I just venture onto someone else's land without permission. The tired looking man at the door thanks me for asking, tells me not to touch his shit, and slams the door.

His shit, I assume, is the rotting copse of vehicles that surrounds the church. It's a reverent congregation of rust and corrosion, intermingled with a gang of stray cats that meet me at the door to the church. One of the cats sits in the entryway; he is missing an eye and a leg and hisses as I try to step inside. He is the pastor now. And I'm not welcome inside.

This pioneer church used to be known as Liberty Church and was constructed in 1871. It was once a picturesque little white church, with a pitched roof and a bell tower. The first pastor was Elder Thomas Jenkins, who served until 1900. At its peak, the church had sixty-six members. The congregation moved in 1922 and disbanded in 1959. That's all I know about this place. I don't know what fights were had between these walls, which couples united in marriage, or which children cried in church and were shushed impatiently by their mothers. Now it sits off Bluff Road, housing an old religion—one of decay and neglect.

Local historians claim this to be one of the first churches in Fremont County, Iowa, built up by pioneers who had come to settle the West. But that's a narrative fiction that presumes America lay empty before the pioneers. Faith has always been part of the American landscape. The question has never been how much faith, but whose.

Liberty Church is adjacent to Waubonsie State Park, named after a Potawatomi chief who fought for the British in the War of 1812.[1] After the war, Waubonsie allied with the United States in order to preserve the life of his tribe. But it was an uneasy peace, shaken by the greedy hands of Manifest Destiny and so many of those white pioneers, who came for free land only to find the ground swelling with the anger of the eradicated. In the self-published histories of some of these early churches, they mention trouble with the Native Americans. In one such history, published by St. John Lutheran Church of Adair, Iowa, the author noted, "no one can realize the hardships endured and the sacrifices made by these early settlers. Wild Indians roamed about in search of plunder."

Of course, it wasn't so simple. It's not plunder if you are reclaiming your home. But that's the story told by early Christian pioneer faith—erasing the faith and spiritualty that existed before.

In the aftermath of the Black Hawk War, Waubonsie was forced to give up Potawatami land in Indiana and Illinois in exchange for a permanent settlement along the Missouri River, and he was given a cabin in the area, northwest of Tabor, Iowa. But after his death in 1848 or 1849, the Potawatami were again forced to move, this time to Kansas. Twenty-three years later, Liberty Church was built—one faith eradicated for another.

Religion for the Potawatami was communal, with groups organized into clans. These clans were the gifts of Wisaka, a hero, who in some traditions was born of a virgin mother and raised by Grandmother Earth. Wisaka was a trickster who created humans from mud. For these original inhabitants of the land, earth and spirit, the divine and the dirt, were inseparable.

Churches expanded on the edges of the frontier in an effort to "tame" the wild lands. These buildings were markers of "civilization" and "progress". Politically, they were also markers of settlement and ownership—an erasure of a past that few of the people in this place remember.

The field of epigenetics argues that trauma is encoded in our DNA and passed down through the generations. If trauma can influence the very composition of our bodies, I wonder what remains in the soil of these ancient hills. I think about this while considering the skeletal siding of Liberty Church, the bones of wood laid bare by time and neglect. Soon this church will dissolve into the stomach of the land. What does it leave behind? What did it take away? And what does the earth remember of these moments of faith both lost and found.

Pioneer churches in the Midwest were more than just places of worship: they were the center of their communities. David Zwart, professor of history at Grand Valley State University, tells me in an email that these early churches are "the heart of the heartland." They were places of physical and emotional support for those lonely settlers, and stories told from the pulpit spun a narrative for those coping with the struggles of frontier life. The story was one of moral superiority, of martyrdom, faith, and hard work. And that's the story that won out. That's the story that Americans are nostalgic for, but it's just a myth.

The truth is that the early settlers were hardly the pious family, bootstrapping it on the prairie. They were instead men with few family attachments, hewing out a living in a strange land in order to escape jail time, debts, and abusive families. In their book *The Churching of America*, Roger Finke and Rodney Stark argue that in 1850, religious adherence on the frontier was weak at best. Iowa had the lowest with 138 religious adherents per thousand of population, and Maryland, Indiana, and Ohio were the highest with 422, 420, and 416 adherents per thousand, respectively.[2]

White American religion then reached the prairie, first through Catholic missionaries and after that with the waves of Methodist and Baptist. The Catholic missionaries themselves were often single men and women. Nuns and monks, who were living in isolation, were supported by a strong centralized church organization. The Methodists and Baptist didn't quite have that organization, but what they did have was disorganization—there was little oversight, little church structure, and as such, the ministers were allowed to adapt to the space and the culture. As Finke and Stark write, "Both denominations developed systems that made it easy for gifted laymen to enter the ministry. Among the Baptists the local preacher, or farmer-preacher, was often a man of local origins, whose call was ratified by his fellow congregants. It was not uncommon for more than one member of a congregation to receive 'God's call.' Those not selected to fill the local pulpit had to seek one elsewhere, typically by starting a new congregation."[3] The Methodists had a system of circuit riders, or itinerant ministers, who served multiple congregations. The result was a land-grab for souls between the two denominations.

Evelyn Birkby's father was one such minister—a Methodist circuit rider. When I visited Birkby in 2017, she was 97 and remembered the Dust Bowl. As we talked, Evelyn sat like a queen in a recliner, her lap covered with a maroon fleece blanket, a butterfly scarf pinned around her shoulders like a cape. Her living room was filled with the fussy tchotchkes of memories and age: small glass pine trees filled shelves near wooden replicas of old-timey schoolhouses and a miniature Flexible Flyer sled, there were hand-painted glass goblets clustered above, mugs of pens, and piles of neatly folded newspapers.

Evelyn lives in Sidney, Iowa, where for sixty-seven years she's worked as a columnist for the *Valley News* in Shenandoah, Iowa, and hosted a call-in radio show called *Up a Country Lane*. Sidney is not far from the Liberty Church and it's Evelyn who told me to visit it; she wanted me to see what's been lost. Evelyn has recently lost a church due to declining attendance—her Methodist church combined with the local Presbyterian church, to create Sidney United Faith.

In an effort to create unity, they built a new church on the edge of town. The building has the white steeple of an older church, but the Berber carpet and vinyl siding of a newer one. In the vestibule, the congregation incorporated the stained glass windows from each church, but everything in the sanctuary is new. Pastor Jason tells me that was intentional: "There was too much history. Too many sacred cows. We had to start over."

Evelyn hates the new building. She doesn't say this outright, she just makes a face when I ask her if she likes it. "Did they have to make it look like that?" she asks. I know what she means. So many of the older Presbyterian and Methodist churches that are scattered throughout the Midwest are made of brick and glass, gleaming oak, and have high ceilings. Newer churches look like warehouses with their cheap vinyl siding and Berber carpet. Some of the hipper churches have taken to using reclaimed barn wood in their interiors, which makes Evelyn laugh. "In my day, barn wood wasn't fancy, it was just trash."

But the beauty of these old churches is also an albatross. Many of them aren't insulated, which makes them expensive to heat with aging boiler systems, and congregations can't afford the cleaning and the maintenance. So many of these churches were built to be beautiful monuments in a harsh environment. But in the middle of America, beauty is often sacrificed for convenience and frugality. So these churches close their doors, sell off their pews, and move into larger more forgiving spaces, ones that are wheelchair accessible. And for all the faces she makes about the design, Evelyn and her wheelchair can actually attend Sidney United Faith.

Evelyn remembers her church as the physical and moral center of the town. When she was a young mother, church was where women shared recipes, and swapped hand-me-downs. It was where they learned who needed meals, who needed help with the babies, and who was having trouble with their marriage. "Honey," Evelyn tells me, "all I had was church. I knew nothing about babies when I first started being a mother. So, I depended a lot on the women at church. We didn't go to coffee together or spend a lot of time on the phone, because we still had a party line then. Sunday mornings were my lifeline."

For a young mother, church was more than religious education—it was her community. "Some weeks, I only left the house to go to church," she tells me. The women in the congregation shared cold remedies for babies, which, according to Evelyn, involved "steam and some molasses." They also shared sleep-training techniques. When I ask her to elaborate, she laughs. "Oh you don't want to know what we did in the old days. We were always giving away zucchini and squash," she says. "Church was our center."

Betty has lived in Iowa her whole life—over eighty years. She told me how she raised three girls in the early 1960s, in a house just outside of Ames, Iowa. "We had one car and [my husband] would take it to work. So it was just me and three babies out there. No one to talk to. No cell phones like you have."

Betty tells me those years were the worst years of her life. And in those years, church was her escape and her sanity. It's not hard to imagine. Even now, so much of Middle America is very rural, and winter's gray desolation and furious blizzards can pen people into their homes for days. The land-scape is deceptively open, but it's easy to get lost and find yourself alone. My first winter with two children, I found myself calling my mom on Facetime just so I could hear an adult human voice. That March, when the last snow-storm hit and we were stuck inside for days, I called my mom crying. "I just need to run away," I wailed. She nodded. She knew. Even with the internet and phones, motherhood is a lonely endeavor. In a snowstorm, it is a whole other level of isolation.

In his novel *Giants in the Earth*, O. E. Rolvaag expresses this desolation of the landscape through the voice of a lonely pioneer mother, writing, "Here was the endless prairie, so rich in its blessings of fertility, but also full of great loneliness—a form of freedom which curiously affected the minds of strangers, especially those to whom the Lord had given a sad heart."[4]

Motherhood on the prairie is not for the faint of heart—either as a turn-of-the-century pioneer or a woman on the edge of town in the 1960s. Church for Rolvaag's characters, and for Betty and Evelyn, proved to be a vital social outlet.

Evelyn was less gloomy than Betty about being homebound and raising three children. Evelyn had three boys and a daughter who died of meningitis when she was two. Church was just as necessary. Not only to combat the ex-treme isolation, but for personal and emotional continuity. Church was more than spiritual development—it was just part of the way things were done. "When we married, we went to church together," explained Evelyn. "When the children came along, we went as a family. It was such a good thing for the boys to grow up with a father who went to church. On Sundays, we went to church. That was just a given. When they got in high school, they didn't want to go to church. But [my husband] would say, I'm sorry, in our family you go to church, and we did. We went to church." But now, that model of faith has changed. Americans don't go to church as often as they used to, or did for a brief period of the 1950s and '60s. And with that change so much has become the same as it was again.

With churches closing, rural protestant denominations have returned to the model of circuit riders—with many Lutheran, Presbyterian, and Methodist ministers having three to five congregations each. They drive their cars from service to service, preaching at one and then continuing on to the next. I visited one of these circuit churches in Thurman, Iowa. It's a small white Methodist church, with gleaming oak floors and a bell still hanging in the bell tower. Marilyn, a woman at the church who has no defined role, but basically runs the entire place, asks me if I want to ring the bell before service. I grew up a Baptist in Texas and my churches didn't have bells. I say, "Yes," a little too eagerly and look for a ladder to climb up to the bell tower. But Marilyn walks me out to the vestibule and unwraps a thin black rope from a metal hook on the wall. The rope comes out through a small hole in the ceiling. I'm disappointed. I don't know what I imagined—something out of a scene from *The Hunchback of Notre Dame*, perhaps? Looking closer, I notice that the hole in the ceiling that this rope hangs through looks as if someone's husband just drilled it with his cordless drill. I can smell the Folgers in the kitchen, where sheets of leftover cookie bars wait for me. And I remember where I am: the Midwest, where everything is practical.

I pull the cord and the resonant *gong* echoes out throughout this town. The bell is an anachronism, a practicality now made quaint. No one needs to hear the bell to be reminded of the service. People have alarm clocks and cell phones. Everyone who is going to attend church is already here.

Time has turned a practicality into nostalgia. But the residents of this town and the people in this church will not let it go. They've let go of too much. And in a world marked by change, the bell stays. In a place of practicality its sonorous clang is a reminder that sometimes continuity is more important than the bottom line.

Tucked in between the Loess hills, Thurman has one gas station, no school, and no post office. There are only 212 residents here. According to census data, the residents of Thurman are commuters; the average time to commute is 33 minutes. Just about how long it takes to get to Omaha. Most of them are married, and with an average age of thirty-seven, I imagine they are all parents tired from a week of commuting, school activities, and sports. Does the bell wake them up and irritate them? Does it remind them of where people expect them to be? Or are they already at another church? Did they drive into cities to attend bigger nondenominational churches where there are drums and scruffy pastors who use YouTube clips and wear flannel? Seventy-five percent of households here are family households. I imagine, if they attend church at all, they go where there is Sunday school and a youth group that goes on retreats.

Today, there is only one child in church—the granddaughter of one of the members, visiting from out of town. Later, Marilyn will tell me that there are many children in this town. To minister to them, the church does before- and after-school care and opens its doors when school has been cancelled because of snow. It helps the parents out. The church, after all, is the only remaining city center in this town that long ago lost its main street.

That's why they keep coming here. The members cannot bear to lose this church, not after they've lost so much. While Thurman has never been big, in the past thirty years they've lost their school to consolidation, their bank to market forces, and their post office to budget cuts. And in 2012, when a tornado devastated the town, they almost lost their church, but the entire town pulled together to rebuild it. They could have razed the building and consolidated with another congregation. The pastor at the time advocated building something cheaper. But after the service, over Folgers with nondairy creamer and Special K bars, Marilyn explains if Thurman doesn't have a church, what is it anymore? Just a collection of houses.

The congregation rebuilt the church and it is beautiful. As we sing "I Stand Amazed in the Presence," the February sun ghosts through the window, floating a perfect halo of light that moves behind the lectern and across the floor. By the time we sing the closing hymn, "Every Time I Feel the Spirit," the light has departed.

Pastor Jan is preaching today about change. She begins her sermon by asking how many people remember a time without electricity. Of the twenty-six people present, thirteen raise their hands: they are all over sixty-five years old. They grew up on farms. Life before technology isn't a distant memory for them—it's a current reality. The church doesn't have Wi-Fi, and many of these homes don't have access to high-speed internet. Despite this, change has come hard and fast. Change, Jan tells the congregation, is difficult. But the Christian life is about change, pain, and transformation. Everyone nods. Their very life is under transformation. Outside the doors of this church, just miles down the road, is a world that looks nothing any of them imagined fifty years ago. We have robot vacuums, Amazon Alexas, and drones for toys. Love, life, and food, all just minutes away by ordering on our phones. But many of the residents here still don't have broadband internet. Change surrounds them, creeping in on the edges, eating away at the familiar fabric of who they are and what they know.

Marilyn tells me she won't get a smart phone—she doesn't think it's good for society with all those people staring at their screens. Another woman, Jean, tells me that she thinks families have the wrong priorities, working all the time instead of staying home with their kids.

I wince at the comment. After all, I'm here working instead of being home with my kids. But I suggest to Jean that perhaps these mothers want to work. Maybe they find value in it?

More value than children? Jean is incredulous. "If you value work more than kids you don't have the right values."

"What about parents who have to work? The economy has been bad, it's hard to have enough money."

Jean again shakes her head. "It's about values."

It's hard to argue poverty with someone who remembers the Great Depression. Jean, Marilyn, Evelyn, they were all raised to be frugal out of survival. The napkins in the church kitchen look like they've been taken from fast food restaurants. They wash and reuse the disposable plastic utensils.

As a teen in South Dakota, I attended a small church. A couple would eat every Sunday at the breakfast buffet of the local Hy-Vee grocery store. The whole breakfast cost no more than five dollars. They got their senior citizen discount and would pay for one meal, the wife eating off the husband's plate. They would keep the plastic utensils from the meal, wash them at home, and bring them back to the church. There was a big cardboard box underneath the church's kitchen sink that held all the reused plastic utensils.

I tell Jean and Marilyn this story and they laugh. "That's what's called recycling," Marilyn explains. "And if we can do that to save money because we have values, surely all these moms don't need to work."

I want to explain to her about work, about how I feel and experience value. I want to tell her how deeply I love my kids and how working isn't a rejection of them but it's an embrace of my life and my skills and oh, by the way, why is it the woman's job anyway? But I can't reargue the entire first wave of feminism in this church. And if I do, it won't help. The line has been drawn at values. It's one word but it means something vastly different to Marilyn than it does to me.

I believe Marilyn is talking in general terms. I think if I told her about my life and my purpose, she'd be on my side. But maybe I'm foolish. And which of us is supposed to bend toward the other? We are worlds away, but at the same table. Between us is an unconquerable space, but for now it's filled with treats, Folgers, and crumpled napkins. I lean forward and listen.

In the next breath, Marilyn is telling me about the church's after-school program. And suddenly our sense of what is a value doesn't seem so distant. Also, the night before was a charity dinner that raised $3,000 for a man, the owner of the gas station, who had fallen on hard times. All the treats we are eating are leftovers from that dinner—cheesecake bars, apple cake bars, Special K bars. And Paul, who runs the after-school program, tells me that the church was able to rebuild because someone in town left enough money in their will for the project. "He wasn't a member of the church," explained Paul, "he just knew that if you lose a church, you lose everything. That's good values."

* * *

The idea of "good values" finds its roots here in the church—in the idea of a Christian protestant ethic. It's both intimately connected with faith, but also has nothing at all to do with faith. It's just as baffling and as infuriating as the land itself, which is both open and exclusionary, adaptable, hard, necessary, and unknowable—open hand and closed fist.

How "good values" are ascertained and defined, determines who is respected, who is hired for jobs, and who receives help. Many of the people in this church are only talking to me because Evelyn vouched for me. I imagine if I had walked in alone with my recorder and my blue hair, I would have been turned away. Even now they are skeptical. I'm a working woman from the big city of Cedar Rapids. My ability to talk about my kids and Evelyn's good word are my only moral capital.

An hour later, I'm back at Evelyn's house having lunch with Pastor Jan. We are having soup, grilled cheese, orange Jell-O salad, and iced tea made from powder. I've never had iced tea made from a powder and it's horrible. It tastes like drinking cardboard. I sip lightly, trying not to choke.

As we talk, Pastor Jan tells me how she came to the ministry, as a second career, after a marriage and a divorce. Of clergy in America, 13 percent are female, but Gallup data from 2015 show that only 5 percent of Americans say that their head pastor is a woman.[5] Jan's current husband is a farmer. They both married later in life and he's supported her in her calling.

But here, where morality is currency and good values are worth more than farmland, I ask Jan if it's hard to lead people who ascribe to more rigid gender roles. Jan makes the point that most of the churches out here are mainline Protestant that have a history of ordaining women, unlike the Baptists (which Evelyn notes as an aside). But there are still few women who actually lead churches.

She often gets calls from women, who, when they hear her voice, ask to speak to the "head" pastor. But she notes without any bitterness that they usually accept her. And even beyond her gender, Jan notes that it is hard being a pastor and it's hard living in Middle America, where people have lost so much—populations, storefronts, schools, and their way of life. Jan preaches to three congregations and spends her days driving all over the county visiting church members who are sick or in nursing homes. Evelyn jokes that Jan should be trained as a nurse, not a minister.

According to US Census data, at nine million the Midwest has the second-highest population of people aged sixty-five and older, trailing the South, which has fourteen million.[6] The Midwest also has high rates of out migration of young people. The role of a minister out here is often to comfort and care for those who are living in a place of remembrance for something that might never have existed.

Evelyn and Marilyn each long for the days when church mattered, when values mattered—when church was indeed the heart of the heartland. But that time is a fiction, perpetuated by political forces in order to fight communism and socialism and bring America together again after World War II.

According to Gallup, church attendance hovered around 39 percent in the 1930s and 1940s.[7] It increased in the 1950s, when Dwight D. Eisenhower encouraged Americans everywhere to go to services. This was the sales pitch: America was now at war with communism, which was perpetuated by atheism. Americans could differentiate themselves from the godless hordes by exercising their freedom of religion. The call was taken up by religious leaders such as Billy Graham, and soon going to church was more than just something for the religious, it was part of being a good American.

Church attendance soared, peaking in the 1960s at 75 percent.[8] Eisenhower was a pragmatist; he didn't care which churches people joined, as long as it was a religion. Religion kept Americans hardworking and preoccupied with values. In her book *The Evangelicals*, Frances Fitzgerald connects this idea of capitalism and Protestantism, through the popularity of Dwight Moody, the famous nineteenth-century evangelist. She writes, "In the United States, as in Britain, the enthusiasm for Moody came in part from the churchmen's sense of crisis about the rapid growth of an impoverished urban working class. The Earl of Shaftesbury, an evangelical Tory and one of Moody's most important English backers, warned that to deprive 'the masses' of 'the checks and restraints of religion' would be to invite Communism, anarchy, and mob rule."[9]

This idea held true almost a century later, when on Labor Day 1957, Billy Graham preached to a Times Square crowd that stretched up Broadway: "Let us tell the whole world tonight that we Americans believe in God . . . that we are morally and spiritually strong as well as militarily and economically."[10] His speech wove Christian faith with economics and politics, creating, in effect, a civil religion, which became less about actual faith and more about defining "American values."

This Gordian knot of religion, faith, commerce, and society is encapsulated in these churches in the heartland: in Evelyn's United Faith Church of Sidney and the United Methodist Church of Thurman. It's also there in the megachurches in the Twin Cities and Chicago and the hip warehouse churches in cities such as Omaha and Cedar Rapids.

In the Midwest, 73 percent of adults identify as Christian: 26 percent are Evangelical Protestant, 19 percent mainline Protestant, 22 percent Catholic, and 26 percent "unaffiliated."[11] These sets of data make up the majority of what belief looks like in Middle America. But I didn't focus on them solely. So much of Middle American can be understood not by who dominates the conversation but by who is pushed out.

But we start here, with these little churches—the vital organs of Middle America. They are the touch points of birth and death, values, and nostalgia. They are more than just centers for faith, they are symbols of continuity in a place that is defined by loss. And these bleeding hearts of the heartland can tell us so much about the forces and currents that are changing our country.

We also start here in Iowa, because there is a mythos about Middle America that provides a narrative through line for who we think we are as Americans.

The Midwest is often ignored by critical trends and vital commerce— the East and West Coasts are continually in a game of "keep away," and the ball tossed between them is power and influence. We are "fly over" country—a place to be from rather than belong to. When stories about economic struggle are reported about the Midwest, the common response is "just move." And so, many people do. US Census data from 2018 shows the Midwest as one of the top places people leave.[12]

But while the power of Middle America might not be in its commercial enterprises or the ready availability of food trends, it is there in the story it tells of America. There is a certain essentialness about the Midwest, and we laud it as a part of a national heritage. The struggling farmer and his alchemy of survival. The mother with her tater tot hot dish. Son playing football. Daughter at dance. Gender norms never challenged. Whiteness never threatened. The sprawl of a yard. Breath. Earth. Space. A sense of easy order. The way things ought to be. The American dream.

In her book *To Serve God and Wal-Mart*, Bethany Moreton writes, "The small farm myth lay at the core of national understanding, enshrined by Thomas Jefferson, the plantation owner who became the republic's third president. Rural Americans had never really dwelt in an Eden of subsistence farming, but small-scale commercial agriculture, in which both production and profits were based in the family, retained an aura praiseworthy Jeffersonian independence. This tradition ennobled all it touched, allowing country merchants and small workshops to present themselves as just a variation on this pattern of American virtue."[13]

The power of the Midwest is that it is the sanctifying myth of America.

Of course, the realities are more complicated than the myth. But that's the narrative that the Heartland offers—pulling its thread between the two coasts. Whenever people ask me if I'm going to move, and I say "no," they quickly note that the Midwest is a "great place to raise a kid." Everyone says that—liberal, conservative, Christian, or atheist. There is a consensus that whatever is here is good; whatever is here is pure, because here we raise food and children. Because here, even in the cities, we are close to nature. Proximity to nature is supposed to mean some sort of purity of heart and mind. Blame it on Thoreau, blame it on Rousseau, blame it on the way that driving down these roads makes me feel closer to something bigger than myself, even if it is just the sky and the land.

But nature is a cruel mother. I live in the second-largest city in Iowa and have witnessed two floods devastate my town. I lost my job after the first flood. Despite crawling through a roof and wading in sewage to save the art in the building. Despite sandbagging the office, watching the slow horror-movie creep of the water.

During the second flood, as I filled sandbags, I was less desperate to save a building and more interested in being there with people. I had come alone and knew no one around me and yet everyone was a neighbor. I saw on their wet strained faces a stubbornness—a hard resolve that must have slid down their double helix from their pioneering and immigrant forebears. An intuition that leans into the forces of disaster with shovels, plows, sandbags, green bean hot dish, lasagna, and grace. I didn't grow up here, but I've carved a space for myself in this world. Here on this edge of human sprawl and nature's resistance. And I've learned that more than anything, this ethos of endurance is a religion. It's a faith that hopes for heaven and prepares for struggle.

During my research, I often bumped against this belief system in a frustratingly fatalistic way. People would tell me that "The kingdom of God was at hand, so . . ." and then there would always be a shrug, which meant what can you do? Why bother saving the earth or mitigating disaster? Why bother banning guns when criminals are everywhere? When the lion prowls outside your door? Why not use more chemicals and feed your family for today, because the future isn't a promise. An insistence that whatever befalls, we endure. Even city people here have a "rural" mentality, which is a fatalism of striving—we work and nature takes. We work and God takes.

When I was twenty-two, I moved to Iowa. That first month as a resident, I went to a potluck and sat with women who were midwives and listened to them discuss the futility of going to hospitals: "If God wants the child he will take it." I almost gasped in horror. Only just managing to shove my mouth full of the homemade bread and keep quiet. But ten years later, I would sit with my friend in her house in Omaha, grieving the loss of her son. And understand that the wisdom of their words wasn't flippant—it was heartbreak. It was a theology of loss—a faith in the inevitability of pain. It's a religion wrought from a hard land.

The heartland is full of faith, both expansive and hard. Both full of beauty and of fatalism. It's an open hand and a closed fist. It's a response to the realities of the land. And in this way it spins a narrative of America so compelling that it's seen everywhere—deep in the West, the South, and Mid-Atlantic. It's there too in the cities, in communities where violence is not wrought from nature, but from the institutions that ought to be protecting them.

After watching the news about a fatal shooting at a church in Texas, a friend asked me why the congregation was responding so callously to the shooting. "Their response seems kind of cliché," she said. "All they do is say 'God will take care of us.'" I recognized her horror. It was the one I had at the potluck of bread with the midwives. I tried to tell her that pain changes you. That loss changes you. That eventually you give yourself over to the forces of God and nature, because here it feels so beyond your control. It's not right, it's not wrong, it's just faith in America.

The thing we always forget about a mother is the same thing we forget about nature—how mean she can be. It's a meanness wrought from too many unidentified labors taken for granted. From a deep misunderstanding of her gifts and powers. This is what we forget about the heartland. Cheesecake, apple bars, hot dish, all rendered in solidarity. Sandbags hefted shoulder to shoulder. Good schools, warm hearts. They come with a rough edge—calloused from so much battling. And maybe this is why I am drawn to this place. I too am tired. But I too won't quit.

Once, after I told a friend how someone I loved called me a heretic and how my pastor at the time had questioned my faith, she said, "I'll never know why you keep believing. Just give up."

"I can't," I said. "It's too much a part of me."

This then is the heart of the heartland. A beautiful, horrible, stubborn faith and it will both destroy us and build us up again.

3

YEARNING FOR BETTER DAYS

Dearest Lord, teach me to be generous.
Teach me to serve You as You deserve:
to give and not to count the cost;
to fight and not to heed the wounds;
to toil and not to seek for rest;
to labor and not to ask for reward,
except that of knowing that I am doing Your will.

Prayer of St. Ignatius for Generosity

ON OCTOBER 22, 1989, JUST OUTSIDE ST. JOSEPH, MINNESOTA, eleven-year-old Jacob Wetterling was kidnapped while riding his bike home from the video store. The case remained unsolved for nearly twenty-seven years, until a local man, Danny Heinrich, confessed in 2016. The Jacob Wetterling case was one of those moments that redefined how Minnesotans saw their small towns. Before Jacob disappeared, people in rural Minnesota believed that they were set apart, special somehow—isolated from all the crime and evil endemic in the cities. But when Jacob went missing, no one felt safe ever again.

I heard about the Jacob Wetterling case when I moved from South Dakota to Minnesota in January 2000. A girl in my high school English class told me the story as a parable, after I told her how I often went for walks alone on the path behind my house. I heard other parents pass the name of Jacob like a talisman to their children when they invoked curfews. If it could happen in St. Joes, then no place was safe. I often hear my friends now, who would be about the same age as Jacob had he been allowed to live, invoking the mythos of "the time before." That remembered time of innocence, when kids were allowed to be kids. When the dangers of kidnapping and murder didn't hide in the bushes of every well-manicured lawn.

Of course, that belief is a lie. Statistically children have never been safer than now. In fact, it's the era when we believed children to be safe that they were the least safe. In the podcast *In the Dark*, journalist Madeleine Baran revealed that before Jacob went missing there was an epidemic of rape and assault among young boys in the area. According to the *Washington Post*, "In 1935, for instance, there were nearly 450 deaths for every 100,000 children aged 1 to 4.[1] Today, there are fewer than 30 deaths for every 100,000 kids in that age group—more than a tenfold decrease."

I think about this case often during the month I spend in Collegeville, Minnesota, on a sabbatical to write this book. St. Joes is just a few short miles away from where I am staying at the College of St. John's. I drive through the town on my way to the gym and the grocery store. One night, a friend and I go into town for a sandwich and coffee. It still feels like a small town, despite the fact that St. Cloud is swallowing it up. The small streets, the charming stores offering flowers and funny cards, the rising spires of the College of St. Benedict. Stepping into this town is like stepping into a lost moment. After eating our dinner of sandwiches, my friend, a Japanese pastor, offered to walk me back to my car. "No, I'm fine," I said. He insisted. It was after nine on a Friday night and I had three blocks to walk. "You think you are safe, and maybe you are. But maybe you aren't, so I will go with you," he said. Everyone wants that time back. But it never existed to begin with.

People and things are always disappearing: boys missing, stores closed, churches closed, schools consolidated. Faith lost. Sixty percent of the people here voted for Trump—they wanted to make America great again. *Again.* They want to step back into a moment—to believe that there was a time before this.

*   *   *

Mark stands with his arms folded against a paling blue sky. Depths of green fall behind him. That's his land. Next to him is a large combine, with its metallic claws hovering above the earth. That's his livelihood. Mark tells me that he doesn't go to church as much as he wants. He has to be here, in his field, working. It's planting season. The spring was wet, so everything is starting a little too late.

It's always something: dry summers, flooding springs, the freeze of early winter. There are also pests and noxious weeds. Every day, he fights and worships nature in equal measure. "Nothing makes me believe in God more than working a field in the early morning," he tells me. He believes in global warming. He believes the world is changing. But he doesn't think we can do anything about it, it's God's will. Mark is a big man, but it's clear he feels small in the context of the capricious beauty of nature.

"Why do you believe in God?" I ask.

"Because if I didn't, I'd have to believe in the bottle."

Too many of the people in this place cope with the constant instability of the land by drinking and using drugs. This is Illinois, where the opioid crisis is in full effect. According to the Illinois Department of Health, "more people died from an opioid drug overdose (due to heroin and prescription opioid pain relievers) in 2014 than from homicide or motor vehicle accidents."[2]

Val Farmer, in his *Rural Stress Survival Guide*, explains the predicament of farmers this way: "There is not a lot to do but worry. Some eat too much, drink too much. Some gamble. Anything to escape from anxiety. . . . No crops, no harvest. No harvest, no income. Short-term notes come due. Nothing to do but wait and worry. There isn't time to do something else, anything else to make ends meet. Belts tighten. No camps for kids. No Christmas. No dinners out. Fewer trips to town. The snowball has started and soon the towns and cities will feel the pain too."[3]

It's a cycle of struggle that breeds nostalgia. And while fewer than 7 percent of rural workers are directly employed in agriculture, the farming mentality directly influences how people in Middle America think and act. In their book *Leading Through Change: Shepherding the Town and Country Church in a New Era*, Ron Klassen, Barney Wells, and Martin Giese note that even in areas defined as cities, a rural mentality can still exist. This "agrarian worldview," as they call it, is pervasive throughout Middle America, and it's defined by a belief in the self, apart from systems and government. And it's a worldview that redefines success, not as advancement but as survival.[4]

The narrative then is one of making do. Where a good year is not one marked by achievement, but simply by staying alive—making moral advances rather than financial ones. Finding solace rather than drive. It's a discourse of loss and a fatalistic language of survival. Who has the capacity to care about climate change when you are barely holding on? A world of survival, financial, emotional, and spiritual, is an anemic place of holding on. Sometimes the biggest freedom is found in your greatest fear—letting go.

It's a moral language I am familiar with. It's one that weaves together the dispensationalism of conservative Christianity with the rural discourse of loss. It's an ideology that says the world is bad, so I tend to my own garden and just have faith in Jesus. It's a political ideology that embraces the inevitable end and looks out only for those things that are believed to be in the individual's control. Which sounds nice, but it's really just a fuck you to the call to love our neighbors as ourselves.

So many of the farmers I meet while researching this book experienced their best years under President Obama. But they voted for Donald Trump in 2016. In fact, it wouldn't be hard to argue that under Obama, farming, at least, was great again. But no one feels that way. Their nostalgia is for something more than monetary gain. It's for something more than better trade deals or a sociopolitical climate that favored corn and wheat prices. And even if things were good, they never trusted it. Plus, even if the money was good, Mark explains, the morality was bad. When I ask what he means, he tells me "abortion and birth control." Plus, all that other good stuff wasn't a result of the policies of Obama. It was just a fluke. He doesn't trust good moments, they go away too easily. It's a poverty mentality born of a reliance on the whims of a capricious land.

Mark longs for the days when his father was a farmer. Things were hard, but life was good. Easier somehow. He's conveniently forgetting the farm crisis of the '80s in order to justify his worldview. In reality, there was never a time when people didn't engage in a relentless battle with the earth. There was never a time when it wasn't hard to be a farmer, or a time when all families were good and moral and Christian. Even the belief in the wholesome rural community is ill-founded. According to *Rural People and Communities in the Twenty-First Century*, rural residents are "more likely to experience chronic or life-threatening illnesses."[5] They are more likely to have cancer, diabetes, high blood pressure, obesity, and mental illness.

While rates of drug and alcohol use overall are slightly higher in metro areas, use among young people in rural areas is significantly higher than among their urban peers. Additionally, according to the Rural Health Information Hub, "A 2010 report to Congress from the Administration for Children and Families (ACF)[6] states that the incidence for all categories of maltreatment was higher in rural counties than in urban counties, with rural children being [two] times more likely to experience harm or endangerment."[7]

I was aware of these statistics as I traveled through the Midwest and often mentioned them in conversation. Everyone thought I was mistaken. Even when I spoke to Barney Wells and Ron Klassen, authors of the book *Leading through Change: Shepherding the Town and Country Church in a New Era* and the architects of a class designed to assist ministers in understanding rural culture, they scoffed at my statistics. I had to show Wells the passage in the book *Rural People and Communities in the Twenty-First Century* (a book he assigned for his class, which I took in July of 2017 and describe in chap. 9) where those statistics were located for him to even consider the possibility. But he challenged the methodology of the researchers.

When it comes to the nostalgia of rural faith, the cognitive dissonance between what is true and what we want to be true is on full display.

* * *

But a belief in nostalgia—in that mythical moment before—is less about reality and more about morality. Jennifer Sherman, in her book *Those Who Work and Those Who Don't*, argues that this sense of rural morality is not about actual morality, but about defiance and opposition. About setting themselves apart from the "other." "Tradition . . . is a protective umbrella under which people can shelter themselves from the worst problems endemic in their community. It simultaneously provides categories according to which they may garner the moral and social standing that comes from embodying its most noble ideas." She also adds that in defining the rural area as good and moral, residents are "able to claim for themselves an identity substantially different from the one that urban and suburban America might impose on them. Instead of seeing themselves as the uneducated hicks and rednecks of the rural stereotypes, they instead construct themselves as morally and socially superior to other groups of Americans."[8] The belief in the goodness of the land and presence of morality is more important than its actuality.

Despite what Biblical literalists believe, the morality of evangelicals is always shifting. For years, evangelicals, Baptists, Catholics, and mainline Protestants supported slavery as God's ordained pattern for the world. And while it's not exactly hard to find slave apologists in America (or on YouTube), you'd be hard pressed to hear the morality of human ownership lauded from the pulpit.

In 2011, only 30 percent of white evangelicals agreed with the statement that "an elected official who commits an immoral act in their personal life can still behave ethically and fulfill their duties in their public and professional life."[9] In 2017, 72 percent argued for the amorality of politicians. In the words of the Reverend Jerry Falwell, Christians were not voting for a "pastor; we're voting for a president."[10] This coincides with over 80 percent of white evangelicals voting for Donald Trump, despite his on-tape discussion of grabbing women by the pussy.[11]

This isn't to say that evangelicals are the only ones with a shifting sense of morality. But rather, the actualities of "good values" and how we remember them are constantly in flux. The pioneers we celebrate as the good-hearted Americans, who pulled themselves up by their bootstraps, also committed government-sanctioned genocide against the Native Americans who populated the land. They were also convicts shuttled west from their cities of origin. People with a good life don't often seek a new one. Even the description of the Midwest as a blank and empty noplace, requires an erasure of truth—the truth of the people and civilization before.

These good values, this good place, this time remembered, is more of a fiction created out of a need to justify ourselves, our presence and our erasure of others. And the narrative that all too often persists in this place is one of family and religion. Of a fatal realism. Of quiet men, whose identity is seeded into the land they own and walk on. Of independence, survival, and belief in the beauty of small places.

It's a mythology born of stern-faced Norwegian, German, and Swedish immigrants, who came here with nostalgia in their blood—yearning to recreate the homeland as they believed it had once been. And it's a nostalgia perpetuated by grandmothers and grandfathers who have pink carpet in the bathroom and Anderson-Erickson sour cream in the fridge, right next to the decades-old margarine container that probably holds fresh potato salad. They remember the Great Depression, they insist that there was a time they remember when things were good—when children went to church, when divorce never happened, when families stuck together.

It would be easy to dismiss this mythology. After all, historians are hard-pressed to find a time in America when life was ever as uncomplicated as we want to remember it. Yet, the ideas that there was a time when Christian faith was more central to the American ethos, and that a person could support his family by simply working the land, do contain a grain of truth. But in this land, truth blends with memory, blends with loss, until the window through which we see the world is dimmed by our myopia.

And it's this nostalgia and creation of a guiding ethic of what we once were that influences the approach to the practical aspects of faith and religion. For example, in many places I visited, there was a focus on schools not scheduling sports and activities on Wednesday nights, because that was traditionally "church night." It is of course, possible to maintain a Christian life and still go to football practice on Wednesday night, but the concern was less about the actualities and more about the nostalgia of the way things "ought to be."

Nostalgia is no small matter. It was the slogan "Make America Great Again" that swept up the people of this region during the 2016 election—tapping into a hope and desire for a past never lived but acutely desired. There was a reason this nostalgia resonated so clearly, because of the deep sense of loss. And the emblem of this mythology is the little white church on the prairie, with its cross sticking up staunchly in the sky.

A study by the Public Religion Research Institute in 2016 found that 74 percent of white evangelicals in the USA believed that America had changed for the worse since the 1950s.[12] According to the PRRI report, "Nearly six in ten white mainline Protestants (59%) and white Catholics (57%) also believe the American way of life has taken a turn for the worse over the past 60 years." Comparatively, six out of ten Americans without a strong religious identity think America has changed for the better.

It's a theology of loss—one that sees as divine all that once was. This belief is one that is intimately connected with the scriptures. After Adam and Eve were thrown out of paradise, the people of God are filled with longing for the return of paradise. Endemic in each of us, the apostle Paul argues, is a collective pain of the loss of what once was.

In Romans, Paul writes, "For the creation waits in eager expectation for the children of God to be revealed. For the creation was subjected to frustration, not by its own choice, but by the will of the one who subjected it, in hope that the creation itself will be liberated from its bondage to decay and brought into the freedom and glory of the children of God. We know that the whole creation has been groaning as in the pains of childbirth right up to the present time" (8:19–22). The loss in this land is entangled with a longing for a misplaced paradise.

I hear this loss when I talk to Evelyn Birkby, who describes in detail the church potlucks with folding tables packed with Jell-O salads and hot dish. I hear this loss too when I hear Mark talk. His voice is sonorous, but his arms are folded. He knows the farm that he has will never be what his father had. He knows he will have little to give his own son, who is studying agriculture at the local state school. "I told him to go into accounting," Mark said. But he smiles, happy creases gather near his eyes. He is proud of the generational continuity. There is, after all, a sweetness to sameness. There is a comfort to this kind of context and continuity—of building a life around relationships rather than ambition.

A new generation of farmers is finding limited success in organic farming. Mark tells me about farmers who become engineers, developing new technologies for seed and pesticide companies. The world is changing. There is hope, but there also needs to be a sense of coherence between the past and the present. Nostalgia can be a toxic force that erases all history and nuance. But it can also be a call to become better versions of ourselves, just like the faith that informs it.

*   *   *

When there is loss and longing, there is also faith to fill in those empty spaces. The result is a complicated morality, which values what once was over what is now. That sees only a divinity in the locked gates of Eden rather than the Kingdom of Heaven here on earth. When I think of the church I created with my friends, I realize now that our competing visions were trapped in a sense of return for them and a hope for something new in me. I had spent so many years marginalized in my faith communities that I wanted to create a new kind of utopia. But the very idea of utopia is ancient, trapped in our concepts of Eden. We didn't want a new heaven and a new earth, we wanted to return to the old, a return to Eden.

During our years of couples therapy, as Dave and I desperately tried to hold together our marriage, our therapist often asked us to tap into that "time before" so we could remember the good things and the good times. Nostalgia here was supposed to be healing. Our work was to make our marriage great again, but at some point even that became an exercise more of myth-making than remembrance. And I didn't want to go back to what was before—I wanted something new. I wasn't happy with what was before.

In *Ignorance*, Milan Kundera writes, "The Greek word for 'return' is *nostos*. *Algos* means 'suffering.' So nostalgia is the suffering caused by an unappeased yearning to return."[13] Kundera then compares the longing to return with the story of Odysseus, a man who reluctantly leaves home and spends a lifetime trying to return. Only when he does return, his home is no longer his home, maybe it never was. For better or worse, there is no return. And maybe there never was an Eden. Maybe there never was a great America. The only option then is to move forward. To change. When I began this book, it was titled *The Death of the Midwestern Church*, which was a title that had been given to a magazine article I had written in 2016. I soon began to hate that title, and I said this to my pastor at the liberal Lutheran church I began attending toward the end of 2017. I was worried it would offend people. Pastor Ritva laughed. "We are Christians," she said. "We believe in death, but we also believe in the triumph over death. If something needs to die, then let it." When the old passes away, when the new arrives, there is pain, loss, grief, and confusion. Even Jesus upon his return from the grave had a new body. No resurrection perfectly quells a grieving heart. Because resurrection is change. Something is different. And nothing can ever truly be the same.

Walking across the St. John's campus one Sunday after Mass, I picked a red berry off of a yew bush. Snow had come early to Northern Minnesota, and in the three weeks I was there as a visitor on campus there had been two snowfalls that covered the earth in thick white beauty, only to quickly melt into gray ice. Snow is a shroud over the ugly death of winter. When it melts, the raw, gray flesh of the world is again revealed. I saw the berries only because it was the first beautiful day in so long and I was walking slowly. Sitting in a Benedictine Mass had overwhelmed me with its sense of eternity. The monks in the mass seemed to be part of an eternal community, each one vital and yet a continuation of a tradition that had begun long before they were born and would continue long after they were gone.

I felt the same sitting in the pew taking part in a liturgy that welcomed me, but didn't need me. I felt like I had been immersed into an eternal landscape of faith. It was the same feeling that comes over me as I drive across the Midwest, as if I'm yielding myself to a land and a place that welcomes me, but doesn't need me. That will continue long after I am gone. That resists the relentless push of humanity in an eternal and relentless existence. Here, land meets sky. Mortal touches immortal. So much is seen and so much is lost.

The Mass had been a drink before war. I would be leaving the campus soon, where I had been cloistered, writing this book. Then, I would have to return to my children, my friends, and the wreck of my life. There would be the holidays to muscle through and relatives to answer to for my broken marriage. I'd have to move out of my house. I'd have to start a new life.

Each task was so monumentally overwhelming, I couldn't even make a list. Instead, I walked slowly and looked at berries on a bush.

I picked one.

As a child, I'd always been warned against bright waxy berries. My mother told me that nature's brightness was a warning of poison and bitterness—bitterness a protection for the seeds inside. But yew berries are not poisonous themselves—it's the small black seeds on the inside. The pine needles of yew also slough off a highly allergic pollen so small it can filter through window screens. Yew trees are noxious to cattle and horses and are often planted as a barrier to keep roaming grazers out. And yet, all is not death with the yew. Extracts of the European yew were used in early chemotherapy drugs, which kill cancer cells in order to save life. Ancient mythology holds that because of the poison of the plant, the yew is a symbol of death. But they are also evergreen, a symbol of eternal life.

It's because of their ambivalent symbology that yews are often found in churchyards. In *Antiquities and Curiosities of the Church*, published in 1897, T. N. Brushfield wades into the confounding symbol of the yew.

> Amongst the ancients the yew, like the cypress, was regarded as the emblem of death. . . . As, to the early Christian, death was the harbinger of life; he could not agree with his classic forefathers in employing the yew or the cypress, "as an emblem of their dying forever." It was the very antithesis of this, and as an emblem of immortality, and to show his belief in the life beyond the grave, that led to his cultivation of the yew in all the burying grounds of those who died in the new faith, and this must be regarded as the primary idea of its presence there.[14]

Death and life. All in one tree. But I wasn't thinking of all of this when I picked the berry. I was thinking about the broken pieces of my life I'd have to pick up when I went home. I was mourning a death, I was longing for a way out. So, I squished the seed out of the flesh of the berry onto the ground. I immediately regretted it. I'm allergic to yews, apparently. My face ached the rest of the day from sinus pain.

Nostalgia works like the yew. It is a protection, but a poisonous one. It offers shield and weaponry, but often turns on those who touch it. It is both everlasting and a harbinger of death. Scottish poet Robert Blair memorialized the yew, writing in his poem *The Grave*, "Cheerless, unsocial plant! that loves to dwell 'Midst skulls and coffins, epitaphs and worms: Where light-heel'd ghosts, and visionary shades, Beneath the wan cold moon (as fame reports) Embodied, thick, perform their mystic rounds. No other merriment, dull tree! is thine."[15] I imagine Blair shouting this and shaking his fist at the yew, his face probably also aching with allergies. Man and nature in an eternal battle. Yew: 1—Blair and me: 0.

When I see Mark, I feel the same overwhelming sense of the eternal as I did in that Mass on Sunday. The cathedral of the sky is his church. We are just part of something bigger here and we both feel it, we are both lost in it, trying to stake our claims in this struggle between us and nature. Nature we realize, will always win. But we wrestle anyway. Finding life in death. Our bodies throbbing after reaching out to touch beauty.

4

THE PEW AND THE PULPIT

A T A BEST WESTERN IN DUBUQUE, IOWA, A group of Lutheran ministers gathers to talk about their churches and communities. The theme is "crisis and conflict," but everyone is genial as they gather around a buffet of deli sandwiches and chicken and wild rice soup. Almost too genial—the line moves slowly because one pastor keeps offering other people her place in line.

"I'm so fine," she says gesturing someone in front of her.

"Oh, I couldn't," the man insists.

They go back and forth until someone from the back of the line shouts happily, "Are you gonna eat or just play nice?" Everyone laughs and the line inches forward. The only thing that would make this more Midwestern would be some tater tot hot dish and for someone to say, "oh geeze"—there are already Special K bars.

The pastors are gathering for the annual Rural Ministry conference sponsored by Wartburg Seminary in Dubuque. The seminary's focus on rural ministry is unique. Mark Yackel-Juleen is the director of Wartburg's Small Town and Rural Ministry program, run through their Center for Theology and Land. They offer a certificate in rural ministry for pastors and lay people interested in gaining a better sense of what it means to live here and a greater understanding of the people and the culture. Yackel-Juleen doesn't believe that there are many programs like his in existence. Not anymore, anyway.

"No one really thinks they are going to be called to pastor in the middle of nowhere," he tells me. But rural churches rank as the highest percentage of Evangelical Lutheran Churches of America congregations.

The conference is a chance for these ministers to gather and talk. So many of them work alone without much in the way of support staff. Others have multiple congregations and spend their days like modern-day circuit riders, traveling through their counties, preaching, drinking some Folgers, and moving onto the next.

It's exhausting and lonely work. A study conducted by Duke University of rural Methodist pastors found that rural clergy take fewer days off and are often paid less than their metropolitan counterparts.[1] But none of the ministers here would trade it for anything. Annie and Lucas, a husband and wife team, share nearby congregations in rural Wisconsin. Neither of them grew up in rural areas, but they both love their congregations and the work.

For them, the conference is a chance to sit and talk shop with other pastors. I sit at a table with pastors from Nebraska, Wisconsin, and North Dakota, and I ask them what the biggest problems are facing their congregation. The first is sports: they can't compete with NFL games, Sunday soccer, and baseball tournaments. The second is politics. Jenny, a pastor of a church in Clinton, Iowa, calls it the "divide between the pew and the pulpit."

The date is March 2, 2017. Every one of the pastors at the table works in a county that voted for Donald Trump, and some are still surprised he won. These are pastors in the ELCA Lutheran tradition, which has a history of affirming women and queer ministers in the pulpit. Additionally, a study of Protestant pastors revealed that over two-thirds have an advanced degree. And studies show that Americans with graduate degrees tend to lean toward liberal politics.[2]

Jenny explains, "Every Sunday I preach about social justice. We raise money for missions and to feed the poor. So many of the people in our community are without health care or are immigrants. I preach compassion for them. But in the wake of the election, it's hard not to feel like the gospel message didn't take." Everyone at the table nods. They are balancing a precarious role—the politics of the pulpit.

Pew and pulpit in America are deeply divided. The ELCA pastors I meet are much more liberal than their congregations. But it's easy to see how this can cut the other way too: pastors more conservative than their liberal congregations. After all, I have spent my whole life attending conservative churches where pastors, without compunction, will tell their congregations that voting pro-life is the only political ethic a Christian must uphold. Only six months before this visit, I walked out of a sermon at a church in Cedar Rapids, Iowa, where the pastor told the congregation that God calls Christians to speak out against gay marriage. When I was seventeen, my parents enrolled me in a camp that was designed to prepare Christian teens for the evil liberalizing influences of college. One of the lessons at the camp was on how the flat tax was the only Biblically acceptable tax. It sounds quaint, but that camp is very much still in existence, continuing to influence generations of Christians.

The Johnson Amendment is a tax code regulation that ostensibly prevents pastors from endorsing a political candidate from the pulpit. But it's rarely enforced and easy to skirt around by pointing out the "correct" morality to the congregation and letting them make the connection in the voting booth. The current president has promised to repeal the Johnson Amendment, and I ask the pastors if this will encourage them to speak out more on issues like social justice and immigration. They all shake their heads. No, they are pastors to *all* people. I respect their morality. I respect their calmness. But I also want to shake them. I want them to use what I see as the "other side's" dirty tactics.

It doesn't feel like a fair fight. Perhaps I'm raw because of the election and because only weeks before this meeting my husband called me a heretic when I defended my pro-choice stance. I'm hurt and angry at a Christian ethic that is so tangled in the politics of the right that voting any other way means that I am seen by my family and my friends as going against the very will of God.

What I feel is the personal impact of the pernicious coupling of religion and politics. This began with Dwight D. Eisenhower, who encouraged Americans to go to church as a way to differentiate themselves from ungodly communists. Billy Graham's political and religious ethics were then taken up by a political organization known as the Moral Majority, founded by Jerry Falwell. I've read many thick tomes that outline exactly how this coupling happened. Those books are pointing out the cultural and historical forces that brought me to this moment, where I am being told I am a heretic by the person who is supposed to love me. It helps me make sense of it, but it doesn't hurt any less.

As a teen in a high school youth group, I was asked by a church leader not to talk about the environment so much. She didn't want anyone thinking the church endorsed that sort of thing. "What sort of thing?" I asked. I knew the answer. I knew that my vocalization of environmental policies would sound liberal in a space where only conservative politics reigned. But I just wanted her to say it out loud. "You know," she said. "Just be good."

One month before the election, I published an article that used conservative Christian arguments to say that the Clintons had a good marriage. One that had persisted through hardship and infidelity. In response to that, a mother at my daughter's school sent me a Facebook message accusing me of not really being saved. She ended the message, "I'll pray for you."

Anyone who lives in the South or the Midwest knows the cloying condescension of the phrase "I'll pray for you." It's the verbal middle finger for the holy types. And then there was the argument not long after, with my husband, where I'd been called a heretic and an idolater for my religious beliefs that included a pro-choice stance. The academic arc of history and politics was no comfort for the pain and separation I felt at the hands of a faith so enmeshed in its own superiority that it had separated me from the life I had built and the people I loved.

Milan Kundera wrote, "How to live in a world with which you disagree? How to live with people when you neither share their suffering nor their joys? When you know that you don't belong among them? . . . Our century refuses to acknowledge anyone's right to disagree with the world. . . . All that remains of such a place is the memory, the ideal of a cloister, the dream of a cloister."[3]

The pastors I met at the conference had, in their way, created such a cloister, a place of peace and rest. I wanted one too. I wanted a fortress against the daily disapprovals that were threatening to ruin me. The ones that were coming from inside my own home.

My friend Nicole is often fond of calling the men in politics with whom she disagrees "the children of God." It's a truth she reiterates to remind herself of their humanity and the leveling forces of faith. But sitting in that Best Western in Dubuque, with the yellow neon of the lights casting us all in a jaundiced glow and with the red and gold medallion carpet, which had seemed grand once to a person picking swatches from a book, I felt no such generosity. Only the smoldering anger of the losses looming over me.

Nine months after I sat with those pastors at their conference, I would move out of my house. The divide in my marriage worsened by the divide in the nation. And only then would it occur to me that my anger at my personal loss and pain was just a mirror image of the losses of the people around me.

As I visited places in the Midwest, I'd heard my own anger in the voice of a dairy farmer as he explained the unreasonable regulations that could shut down his farm. His whole livelihood could be shattered by a rule made by someone he felt understood nothing of his life. In the days before I moved out, I too would tell my husband that he knew nothing about me. But the problem for both me and the dairy farmer was that the rules and judgments that threatened to crush us were made by the people entrusted with our protection. What recourse had we then? What faith in the other? And then, what hope that we could crawl out from underneath our burdens?

But again, back to that hotel dining room, with its Band-Aid beige walls and understated chandeliers. It was a decor designed to fit whoever came in: a wedding party, an American Legion luncheon, a convention of pastors. But in its forceful attempt at grand neutrality, the room was offending all my senses.

The politics dividing the congregations of these ministers were complicated. Many of the pastors in the room didn't grow up in the communities they served. They are outsiders, and even if they stay in those towns for their entire career (statistics show this is rare), they might never gain insider status. And as such they are treated with an ambivalent mix of hospitality and isolation. The extremes of people and place exist everywhere, but here in Middle America there are fewer people and places and institutions to mediate those tensions. So the extremes rise up sharply into our lives and communities, threatening to ruin us. And sometimes they do.

These are the frustrations of the people who live here with the depictions of the Midwest. We are conservative, but also very liberal. We are farmers, but we are also business people. We are the place people are often from, and yet not the place to move to. We are the connective tissue between the coasts, but are often flown over. Resisting representation, caught between the extremes, we are seen as a void—a "great desolation" wrote the novelist O. E. Rolvaag. But that's the biggest mistake people have been making about this great middle place since America was first settled—assuming that it's empty.

This place has always been full. Full first of Native Americans who were violently eradicated from the land. It's full now of people who feel like they are being slowly bled from the place to which they belong. Ignored. Misunderstood. But also not seeking to understand. Not seeking to be understood. It's a stubbornness that takes on a language of eternity: journalists will come and go, so will pastors, and so too will many of their children, but the people who are here will remain. So let the trends pass by—the gourmet cupcakes, the silly shoes, Zumba classes, drums in the church, and the electric guitars.

I think often of Evelyn Birkby's eye roll when she talked about pastors who come to these towns with their plans to "revitalize" the church. How many plans for growth from strangers has she seen? How many men and women have walked into her town with plans to change and walked out of that same town with everything the way it has always been. As Americans, we are addicted to growth. But ask Evelyn and she'll tell you: What will grow here, will grow, but only with tenacity and the sun and rain. And you can't control the weather.

These ministers with their outsider status feel these extremes as they speak and lead a congregation that often feels oppositional to them. Mark Yackel-Juleen tells me that single women ministers are often sent to these rural places where they experience isolation as outsiders and as unmarried women, and even more so if they are also queer or a person of color. Additionally, their salaries come at the will of the congregation. One pastor at the table tells me that she has had more than one member of her congregation threaten to withhold their money out of frustration with the changes she's been initiating—namely, streaming her sermons on Facebook Live.

These divides have been in place for decades, of course. But they feel more immediate in this time, as the news fixates on our divide. America is divided, I hear and read over and over. I read a book that promises to provide much needed insight into the American divide, but all it tells me is that there is a divide. I read another book, this one more famous—a best seller—about the rural South. But it peddles in stereotypes and judgments about conservative voters.

Later, on another trip, this one with Catholics in Irene, South Dakota, I strike up a conversation with a woman in the chip aisle of the local grocery store. I tell her about the famous book that's supposed to explain America's divide. I tell her it's a best seller and that it was written by someone in a tech job and ask her if she's read it. She's got three kids and a full-time job and doesn't have time to read that nonsense, but she tells me it "sounds terrible."

"I know," I tell her, defeated. "It is."

"Then why read it?"

"I guess I want to understand," I say and gesture around me. She rolls her eyes and scans the potato chip selections in my hands and says, "Well, I want a yacht."

It strikes me how unconcerned she is. So many people want to understand her and the people around her. She doesn't give a shit. And I wonder if maybe the divide isn't a little overstated—after all, we are here in this chip aisle talking like friends.

* * *

The politics of the pulpit are more complicated than the 2016 election would have us believe. Two-thirds of Catholics and mainline Protestants support gay marriage, along with 35 percent of white Evangelicals.[4] The numbers are not overwhelming, but research shows that the number is growing. Although Evangelical churches are loosely formed coalitions, the Evangelical Free Church of America has taken a strong stance against same-sex unions.

There are other breaks in the politics of Christianity. In February 2017, more than five hundred evangelical pastors and ministry leaders from all fifty states signed a letter critical of President Trump's immigration ban against Muslims. Another petition against that same ban was signed by over eight hundred mainline Protestant ministers. In contrast, a Pew research poll showed strong support for the president's ban among white evangelical Protestants, with 76 percent reporting that they approve of the ban. Among white mainline Protestants, 50 percent approved.[5]

The area between the theology of the pulpit and the beliefs in the pew is a dissonant space. Of course, it's unreasonable to assume that Americans have ever moved in lockstep with the beliefs mandated by their churches. But because of the twist of politics and faith, it's a discord we must reckon with every day.

"I'm not political," my friend at the gym told me immediately after the election. We are both white women, we are both mothers, both Christians. She was telling me this because I was wearing a shirt that read, "Nasty Woman." I'd bought it right after the debates from one of those links that a friend tweeted; the proceeds were supposed to go to a good cause. But I hadn't worn it until now, because I was afraid of tripping off yet another political land mine in the vast desert that lay between me and my husband.

"I'm trying to work out," she told me pointing to the shirt. "This shouldn't be a political space."

But everything is political if you don't fit in. The idea of political neutrality is an idea born of privilege, born of bodies not always under assault from the laws and eyes that decide what is normal and what is protected in this country.

Immediately after the election, people in gyms across America were having this same argument. News stories reported that people who wore

Trump T-shirts to gyms had complaints lodged against them. One news story told of a gym that took out its televisions because people on the treadmills were getting in fights over the news.

I switched gyms that summer to one that had no TVs. It was a boutique gym, where exercises were led by fitness instructors and loud music drowned out conversation. But the gym was expensive, and it was a political respite I was able to afford through my privilege, which in and of itself was political. Even when I ran on the roads early in the morning, I felt the politics of my body in America wash over me. I ran with mace to keep away rapists. Men catcalled me from the road. I ran on sidewalks and bike lanes newly installed with money from a controversial tax.

Everything is political. The only people who could pretend otherwise are people who can afford to hide from it. In these churches too—while "Make America Great Again" hats and "Nasty Woman" T-shirts, for the most part, stay outside the doors—the politics of who was there and who wasn't sitting with me in the pews remains a persistent reality.

Immediately after the election, as news media and *SNL* skits lambasted liberals for living in an "isolated bubble," I found myself wishing for exactly that. "What's so wrong with a liberal bubble?" I asked friends in New York. "They sound nice." The truth was, I too longed for a cloister in a world that seemed to broker no disagreement. Divides hurt. But I needed to divide and separate, in order to heal.

* * *

While Christian faith culture in America is still largely conservative, there are signs that things are changing, despite what those pastors said in the Best Western in 2017. An article in *Publisher's Weekly* from March 2018, outlines a trend in religious books that read as politically liberal—challenging the conservative influence of Evangelicalism. The article summarizes the books, noting that "Religions can be the cause of oppression and injustice, but they also will be part of the solution. Many authors have diagnosed religion's ills and offered cures, in books from religion publishers on topics such as the conflicts over Trump's agenda, urgent social problems, the fragmenting of American churches, and the continuing decline of commitment to traditional faiths."[6]

After the conference, I reached out to some of the pastors from that 2017 meeting and asked them if they had become bolder in speaking out against political issues. Jenny told me that while she was still a pastor to all people, she had begun being more politically explicit in her sermons. But she didn't see her sermons as political—she wasn't speaking about liberal or conservative, she was speaking out for justice. An issue that all Christian's could agree on.

The pastor of the Lutheran church I attend, Pastor Ritva, told me she'd noticed a similar trend in her sermons. She's always been an activist, but she says she's been challenged to speak up more against the injustices she sees being committed in Christ's name by our current political leaders.

It might not be enough to move the needle, but Roger Finke explained in an email to me that radical movements are often inspired by religious teachings. "'Radical' movements often rely on religious beliefs to effectively mobilize a population. During the twentieth century, 'radical' Catholic movements mobilized groups in Ireland, Quebec, and Poland," he wrote.

And religious movements in America have always gathered strength by being on the fringes. Finke and Rodney Stark point out in their book *The Churching of America* that for the most part these movements have been conservative. But the narrative might be flipping. But even if it does, that still means that faith and politics are braided together in a pernicious and difficult union.

* * *

Several months after I moved out and filed for divorce, a friend of mine sends her father over to my house with a chair from her house. I don't have much furniture in my new place and she has too much, she tells me. Instead of bringing me the hand-me-down chair, however, her father brings me a brand-new chair he bought just for me. It's leather and it's gorgeous. And I'm shocked.

I've never met this man before. He's a local business owner and a very conservative Catholic. I worry that he might judge me—he knows I've moved out and filed for divorce. But two of his daughters have divorced, he tells me. He says in a year I'll be doing better than before. He says it's hard, but he loves my writing, he knows I'll come through. While he moves the chair in, he jovially remarks on the sign in my dining room that reads "Resist!" and I'm embarrassed by his generosity, my politics and poverty. The only thing I have to offer him is a box of Girl Scout cookies, which he accepts gladly. The next day he sends me a picture of the cookies cut up into letters that spell "Resist."

The hilarity and kindness make me cry. This feels the most like a Christian thing anyone has done for me in a while. He is a stranger who, because of the nature of the Midwest, knows me, knows all about my mistakes and my mess, who might even fundamentally disagree with my politics, but here he is, generous and kind, reassuring and self-effacing.

When we talk about divide, we also have to talk about union—we have to talk about the messy meetings between strangers and the outpourings of love. We have to talk about strangers standing in pews next to one another, singing the same songs, saying the same prayers, offering one another handshakes of peace, sharing bread and wine—and even if all of these small rituals mean different things to each person, we are there together offering ourselves in messy and holy community. After all, pew and pulpit may be divided in America, but so is the pulpit with the pulpit and the pew with the pew. But we are all inside the same building.

5

THE CHURCH OF THE AIR

Angela Herrington believes in reclaiming lost things—her life, her faith, and Facebook. A Gen-X mother of five and a former nurse, Herrington graduated in April 2017 from Indiana Wesleyan University with her master's of divinity. But her calling isn't to lead a congregation in a church; rather she's leading a congregation online. Herrington is the founder of "Broken, Beautiful and Bold," a Facebook group dedicated to training women to be leaders in the church. The group has a Facebook page with over seventy-two thousand members that operates like a church community for women seeking a place to practice their faith and discover their spiritual calling.

"The great commission for a lot of people means knocking on doors and handing out tracts," explains Herrington referring to the New Testament passage in Matthew where Jesus tells his follows to "go make disciples of all nations." "For me, the great commission is getting on Facebook and telling the woman who is homeless and scared to death that her daughter is going to be taken away that it's okay, that we're praying for her. That's the great commission to me."

The Facebook page is an open community, operated by Herrington and a group of volunteers. Women go there to talk about their faith and encourage one another. The wall is full of supportive memes and cries for help. One post from a member declares, "Girl, you fab!" Another post questions God's faithfulness in a difficult time. Herrington also posts messages, memes, and videos of herself offering short homilies of encouragement infused with a Christian message of God's grace and redemption.

Herrington's group is one of thousands of Christian communities woven into the fabric of technology and social media. Apps such as She Reads Truth offer women Bible studies on the go, the First5 Bible study app offers a group forum, the Sacred Ordinary Days online community is a companion to their liturgical journal. A countless number of Facebook groups, Twitter DMs, message forums, and Gmail threads offer women a private space in which to share the cries and desires of their heart. It's what church should be—they offer one another support and love, raising money for people in need, celebrating births, and mourning deaths. Most of the groups are organic—not sponsored by churches or ordained ministers—springing up from a mutual desire to connect and discuss faith in a private and nurturing environment. Many of them are run by women, like Herrington, who come to faith and ministry as a lay person.

As part of her master's program, Herrington studied her community extensively and found that the women who are drawn to her page are frustrated with the existing church structures. In Herrington's study, 22 percent of women felt undervalued by their Christian community, compared to 16 percent feeling undervalued by their non-Christian communities.

The feeling is understandable. The Christian church, which proclaims freedom through faith, still clings to deeply ingrained misogyny. A study by an Evangelical research organization, the Barna Group, found that only 9 percent of pastors in American Protestant churches were women.[1] Many denominations, such as the Evangelical Church of America and the Southern Baptists, refuse to ordain women. And where there are opportunities for practicing faith within the structure of the church, there is often unchecked sexism and bias. Many women in Herrington's study noted that they felt confined to serving only in children's ministry, which is a pink ghetto for many churches and denominations.

One woman in Herrington's survey, who was allowed to volunteer at her church at a higher level, found herself shut out of key meetings and conversations, "finding out after the fact that conversations [were] happening around tables far away." For women like this, and so many others, social media functions as an outlet that works outside the traditional four walls of the church to unite women in community, purpose, and faith. They are renegade churches, conducted on the internet, where women find themselves valued, listened to, believed, and understood.

There is no number to put on these groups either official or organic, but I don't know a woman of faith who hasn't been a part of one at some point. And this is significant because in the United States, 87 percent of women believe in God, 50 percent read the Bible once a month or more, 82 percent describe religion as somewhat or very important to their lives, and 73 percent attend church services at least once a month.[2] These online groups form an outlet for their faith that these women cannot find offline. Kristin, a member of three such groups, told me that they have been her lifeline in a way that her own church has failed to be. Stephanie explains how podcasts and the communities created around them have given her a chance to explore her faith outside the confines of her conservative church. Knowing that there are other women out there who believe like she does and question the same things she does has given her the confidence to find a new way to practice her faith.

Like the scrappy pioneer churches of the American West, these online spaces are run by religious autodidacts, who pull together makeshift homes for their faith, from the stuff off the internet. Where communities were once hewn from local lumber and hammered together in communal church raisings, women now build their faith spaces with words, moderation, lines of code, jpgs, gifs, and heartfelt outpourings clacked out on thousands of keyboards around the world.

* * *

Herrington does most of her work in a reclaimed storefront in Marion, Indiana. It's a coworking space owned by a faith-based nonprofit. The space has high ceilings and wood floors that glow with a luster of varnish. Inspirational quotes on imitation barnwood hang on the walls. Fliers for Bible studies are pinned to a corkboard that's framed with distressed wood. "The space is faith-based, but everyone is welcome," Herrington explains. It's the motto of Herrington's faith as well. As we talk, a torrent of rain falls on the empty downtown streets that the city is desperately working to revive.

All towns in Middle America seem, in their own way, caught up in this cycle of death and revival. My town, Cedar Rapids, had a devastating flood in 2008, after which we had the money, grants, charity, government aid, and the inspired community will to invest in an indoor market and an ultra-modern coworking loft. But Marion's undoing has been a slow erosion by opioids and addiction.

It's a decomposition that Herrington understands. She had what she calls a "prodigal season." When she became pregnant, she dropped out of college to marry the father of her child. Three years later, she was divorced and struggling with depression and thoughts of suicide. She moved back in with her parents and went to nursing school. She met her current husband, and together they started going to church. They wanted to give their children a faith, something to hold them steady in the tempests of life that they knew too well.

They began going to a small rural church just outside of Marion. "All churches are rural in the Midwest," Herrington quips, laughing at a joke that is funny precisely because it's true. Rural is an ever-shifting concept, influenced by context. The town of Marion has a population of thirty thousand and is the county seat for Grant County in Indiana. For many, it's the big city, but when Herrington and I try to find a restaurant open for a late lunch, we only have two options.

At her first church, Herrington found solace in her faith, but she also felt like something was missing, something she couldn't describe until she heard the voice of God calling her into ministry. For Herrington, 2008 was a year of personal crisis. Her great-grandmother died in June and her father-in-law died the following month from cancer. At the end of the year, her daughter Mary was born and Herrington celebrated new life with the New Year. But three weeks later, Mary contracted a severe case of respiratory syncytial virus (RSV) and stopped breathing. She survived, but Herrington needed a vacation. She took her family out to the Acadia National Park, and it was there she felt called to go into ministry. It was a lot like a road to Damascus experience, if the apostle Paul had had an infant in an SUV and knew about the internet.

Driving through the forest after dropping off her husband and sons for a fishing trip, with baby Mary in the back seat, Herrington heard the words, "You are supposed to go into ministry." So, when she got back home she started blogging. She knew she had to blog because she wanted to reach people who would never set foot inside a church, a hesitation Herrington understood full well from her prodigal days. It's not that she wanted to supplant the church, but she knew that the church was missing something—something real and vital.

She still has a hard time articulating what that "thing" was. She begins by describing how raw her life has been. "I've battled depression and suicide my whole life. No matter how compassionate someone is toward me, if they don't have that in their wheelhouse . . . I just didn't feel like I fit in." It was an invisible wall that felt to Herrington almost like a cultural divide. A gaping silence between the parts of her that her church saw and the parts of her that she needed to bring into the light. "I'm Gen-X through and through, I'm not keeping that crap in the closet, because if somebody else had shared their struggles with me before I had my struggles, I might not have come so close to dying."

And just by sharing her life on Facebook, Herrington catalyzed a new church into being. It happened by accident. She set up a Facebook page under her name for her blog and soon discovered that the page was becoming more popular than the blog. Writers, other bloggers, and Bible study leaders—all women—began to like and share Herrington's regular posts on faith and life. The women who come to her page have varying levels of faith and involvement in their local churches, but they all feel, like Herrington, that something is missing there. Herrington's online community fills that void offering women a chance to be their full selves, fully appreciated, listened to, and valued.

Most of her online followers live in the middle of the country—a swath spanning the Midwest down into Texas. Places where 26 percent of people are Evangelical Protestant, a designation that includes the most conservative of protestant denominations such as Southern Baptist. And 21 percent are Catholic. These are faith traditions where women are often barred from higher-level service roles, relegated to the nursery, the coffee bar, or women's ministry. Women who are otherwise allowed positions of power in their careers and personal life are finding themselves discriminated against at church. "There are amazing women who only want to work in the nursery," said Herrington. "They're the best at it, but don't put me in the nursery. I did my time with my babies. And I love babies, but you give me eight of them? That's not my gift."

Groups like Herrington's provide spaces online where women are allowed to teach, question, and explore theology in their own way, outside of repressive structures. So many of the women Herrington spoke to in her group also found validation in the knowledge they weren't alone in their frustrations with their churches. "When people start reading some of these interviews, they're like, 'Oh my god, that's me.' That makes it a systemic issue rather than a flaw in me or, 'I'm just not good enough.'"

Although she has her master's from a denomination that ordains women, Herrington is hesitant to be formally ordained. She values her role as an outsider, describing the groups of women who meet through the internet as little pockets of "freedom fighters" communicating and organizing to change the church from the outside. "We don't have to change the most conservative fundamentalists," Herrington acknowledged, "we just have to give the people who question them space to do it in a safe way. It's the whole, if she can see it, she can be it. And maybe what we need to see is women as creative, resourceful, and whole and equally loved by God, because if you've been given all these gifts, and you're not allowed to use them in your church? Well, does that make those gifts a mistake?"

Change is happening, but happening slowly, especially in the heart of America where faith saturates every filament of life—from which school activities happen on a Wednesday night, to when and if restaurants are open on a Sunday. While overall, 79 percent of Christians, Protestants, and Catholics in America have said they are comfortable with a female pastor or priest, 61 percent of Evangelicals said they were uncomfortable with the prospect of a woman in the pulpit.[3] And in the Evangelical stronghold of America's heartland, these opinions have devastating consequences.

I've known Kristin since I was in sixth grade. We met at a Baptist church in South Dakota, and grew up together, often having sleepovers on her parent's acreage, where she became a teenage Dr. Dolittle to a menagerie of raccoons, pigs, llamas, cats, and a pack of the friendliest, fluffiest golden retrievers. After graduating from Iowa State, Kristin became a veterinarian and opened her own practice in Omaha.

When I was starting my church in Cedar Rapids, Kristin and her husband joined a start-up church in Omaha. The church was nondenominational but had what Kristin sensed were deeply conservative foundations. Still, she and her husband loved the community they discovered there, and Kristin found a calling in organizing the children's ministry.

Kristin believed that although she and the church leaders might disagree on their approach to things like women's leadership, they were united in journeying together on the issues. Several times, Kristin mentioned to the pastors her disagreement with them on political issues. And each time, they seemed to reaffirm to Kristin that while they may not agree, they were committed to exploring the issues with an open mind and to listening to one another in a community of faith.

Right before the 2016 election, the pastors began a sermon series, preaching against what they saw as the moral decline of America, taking a strong stand against political issues such as abortion, gay rights, and women in leadership. This bothered Kristin, but when she tried to set up a meeting to talk to the head pastor about the sermons, she was told that he wouldn't meet with her without her husband present. When they finally all met to discuss the issues, the pastor told Kristin and her husband that if they disagreed with the church then they were welcome to find a new one. "It was devastating," Kristin said of the experience. "I put my whole life into this church, I built their children's ministry. But when it came to this moment, they wouldn't even listen to me." Used for her labor and then ignored—it's the story of so many women in churches.

Kristin and her husband have decided to find a new church. Raised Evangelical, they are now trying mainline Protestant denominations and churches with more liturgical traditions. As they began to search, Kristin found herself seeking out alternate forms of faith community online. It's a DIY kind of Christianity. But one that allows women to find freedom in conservative spaces.

* * *

In the summer of 2013, after the closure of a church I helped start, I told my husband I didn't know if I ever wanted to attend church again. I had wanted to create a community of faith, focused around inclusion and helping the community. But the reality became something far different—we were a community that mimicked a dysfunctional family. Our pastor berated people he believed were not contributing, while our elders remained silent. People would come through our doors and offer to help but would be immediately turned away by our pastor who warned against people "co-opting our agenda."

I was only three weeks pregnant with my first child when our church started, and when it closed my second child was a year old. Lost in the fog of early motherhood, I struggled to pull our church back on track, sending emails during late-night breastfeeding sessions and hosting meetings in my house while my kids slept. In the end, when finally I was able to call a meeting to address the issue of Adam wanting to take over a local Methodist congregation, the mess of our church was too far gone.

We were sitting in a circle in the church building, which was an old railroad depot and had been a pet store before we put in carpet and converted it to our church. The chairs with their padded mauve seats had been salvaged from a doctor's office creaked as I leaned backward in my seat. I had been told I had no authority.

"When was that decision made?"

The circle looked at me, silent. In just a few days, we would vote to close the doors, but we didn't know that then. I didn't feel like I was in a circle of friends—people who had brought me lasagnas and tater tot casseroles after each birth. I felt like I was in a group of strangers. When had these decisions been made? What sort of silent agreement among the men had been struck? How had I missed it? Our pastor cleared his throat.

"It's a Biblical principle and we agreed to found our church on Biblical principles."

"That hardly seems fair, it's an interpretation. I never agreed to that interpretation, I . . ."

I looked around the circle. Only my friend Mattie nodded in agreement. The rest of the couples and my husband all looked at me as if from behind a wall. I'd given up time and money for this church. I'd spent late nights on the website and in Jim and Susan's basement, going over plans and drinking cheap wine. I believed, lived, and worked as if I was co-equal in an enterprise that never intended to fully include me, that had never been structured to listen to my voice.

Three days later, we voted to close the church. Four days later, the head pastor, Adam, sent an email berating my lack of faith in the word of God.

After all of that, I was done. No more church, not ever. For my whole life I've attended churches in the middle of the country: in Texas, Iowa, Minnesota, and South Dakota. Even the church I had built had become a place where I was rejected and my voice was silenced. I was done. My friend Anna told me, "If the car breaks enough, you trade it in." The car was so broken that I was ready to give up driving.

I told my friend Nicole about my experience and she invited me to an email thread. Dubbed "the God thread," the goal was to be just a group of women of faith who wanted to talk about it. I joined. That small folder in my email, dedicated just to "the God thread," has done more for me than thirty-five years of church attendance. That one email thread wirelessly commingled technology with my pain and heartache, creating that space in the invisible network of Wi-Fi and air for my doubt, anger, and faith.

For so many women, our voices are silenced in the very places where we need to cry out. Where does our pain, or invisibility, have to rest its head? To where can we bring this baggage when even the pastors tasked with caring for our hearts, tell us to be more quiet, more submissive, and as a result moderate every expression of our pain? To the air. To the network. To the complicated connections of wire and air. At least for now, that is. At least until we can regain our footing.

Other churches are experimenting with social networks as an outgrowth of faith communities and not their replacement. Angela Herrington doesn't want to be a substitute for church. While she believes that church is anywhere God is, the goal of her online community is to augment the work of physical churches—encouraging and equipping women to go back to the physical homes of their faith and challenge the biases and assumptions that keep them silent. If it sounds like war, it is. It's a guerilla war designed to take the church back. "In war, how do you battle?" She asked. "You split forces and isolate people."

And it's easy to feel isolated on the prairie. Driving home to Iowa from Marion, Indiana, I went through Chicago, sure, but it was far easier to find a field than a town. Far easier to find empty spaces than people. Even in my town, Cedar Rapids, the second-largest city in Iowa, you are never more than minutes from a cornfield. It's a bigness that can feel limiting if you are the only one of you that you see. But the internet is an equalizer—bringing together voices that once felt alone, realigning boundaries, creating spaces where there were none before.

There is a danger too of creating ideological bubbles. Of filtering out dissent. It's a criticism that was leveled heavily against blue states after the 2016 election. But when you are in the minority—the voice that is silenced— you are never in a bubble, even if you try. And finding a place where you don't have to fight for acceptance, where you can just be accepted, even if that is online is the difference between pain and hope.

But although these networks feel like a solution, they aren't always accessible. In the United States, 4 percent of people in cities don't have access to broadband, but in rural areas it is 39 percent.[4] That adds up to about twenty-two million people. But those estimations, according to the broadband advocacy nonprofit Connected Nation, are wildly inaccurate. The reality is even worse and the data grossly inaccurate. Basically, the FCC requires providers to report their coverage areas as broken out by census blocks. In cities, these census blocks are often actual neighborhood blocks. But in rural areas they can be quite large. If just one house in that area is served by a provider, then the FCC considers the entire area connected.[5]

And even if rural communities do have access to broadband, it is prohibitively expensive for places where the average income is a lot lower. Cell phone data isn't an answer, as coverage in rural areas is spotty at best. And data plans cost money too—a lot of money. With the rollbacks of net neutrality laws, which sought to establish fair and equal access to the internet for all, the future of how people access vital communities and information is at stake.

On November 8, 2016, I babysat for my friend and neighbor Stephanie, so she could go to the polls. She is a mother of four children. She was raised in the Deep South, she homeschools, and she is Evangelical. Her opinions had often chafed against my own during our six years as neighbors, and I was pretty sure she would be voting the exact opposite way I wanted her to. But I believe in voting, so I offered to watch her kids. Eighteen months later, she texted me to tell me about this online community she'd joined. She told me that in the past year and a half, she found herself questioning her church after being told over and over again by her pastor and Bible study leaders that she was too demanding and domineering in her home. "Turns out, I'm just a leader," she told me. "That's not a sin." One day, in the suggested groups section of Facebook, Stephanie saw a group called "Heretics." Drawn in by the tongue-in-cheek name and seeing women in there who she recognized as friends, she joined the group. From there she began listening to podcasts, reading the books suggested by the members of the group, and joining other groups. Emboldened by this new community, she stopped going to her conservative church and has found peace and faith outside the rigors of the institutionalized and spiritualized misogyny that told her she should quiet down and let men be in charge. She's not ready to go public with her beliefs, but the privacy and comradery of these groups is a godsend to her and other women who feel misunderstood and unseen by their faith communities.

These tiny little churches of women that connect through the air are weird, radical, and haphazard but have the power to change.

6

ROOM AT THE TABLE

[The kingdom of heaven] will not come by watching for it. It will not
be said, "Look here it is," or "Look there it is." Rather the father's
kingdom is spread out upon the earth and people do not see it.

Jesus, quoted in the Gospel of Thomas

THE MIDWEST HAS A TERRIBLE OPENNESS TO IT. It's an openness that
can absorb you and lose you. It's an emptiness that can terrify and ex-
hilarate. I love it and hate it in equal measure. I didn't grow up in the Midwest; I grew up in Texas, where the openness of the land sprawls hard and
wide—like a big, calloused hand. There, people stretch rather than cluster.
The weather rarely gets cold. Blizzards don't blow piles of snow against doors
and windows, so there are fewer windbreaks and less grace in the geography.

I moved to South Dakota from Texas right before I turned thirteen.
In November of 1995, my family drove up from Dallas to Sioux City. We'd
stayed overnight in Kansas, and when we arrived in Sioux City I had not
left the car since Nebraska. At our hotel in Sioux City, I stepped outside and
my face began to sting with a thousand tiny stabs of ice that blew through
the air. I hadn't even seen the snow through the car window. The world just
looked as if a gray haze had settled over it. My sister, who had just gotten
braces, screamed. The bitter subzero winds froze the metal in her mouth.

"Snow," my mother said cheerfully as she rushed us into the hotel lobby.

"This isn't snow," I grumbled. "This is torture."

My ancestors, I am told, emigrated from Poland and settled on the East
Coast. They never made it farther than that. There is a story about my great
grandfather blowing up his sharecropper's cabin with a homemade still.
The other side of my family came from English colonies, on the "second

Mayflower" my grandmother always liked to brag. They stayed in Virginia fanning themselves on porches.

Sweet tea and moonshine run through my veins. I am not of pioneer stock. My body has not been carefully winnowed through natural selection to survive here in this frozen vastness. After we moved from Texas to South Dakota, my family spent the entire winter sick with pneumonia and dry, racking coughs. Five years later we moved to Minnesota, and then I moved with Dave to Iowa. But my body never really acclimates. I don't know how to be stoic when wind slices my face with subzero temperatures. I don't know how to ski. I hate the cold and I've never found a way to stay warm in a Midwestern winter.

By contrast, in the Midwest, everyone seems built for the cold prairie. Thick necks, thick legs, thin lips. strong legs—it's the DNA of survival made manifest. All those survival tricks passed down from generation to generation—plastic bags over socks, before you put them in your boots. Washing Ziplocs, storing away apples. Trying again and again after flood and locusts and drought. There is a sense of cheery surrender to the fatality of the land. "Oh well, God willing next year . . ." is something I hear over and over, from people who live in cities and on farms. It's a gut-level acceptance of the Sisyphean task of remaining in a place that has been occupied for centuries and still has yet to be completely settled. Where families have lived for generations and never mastered the earth around them.

"Why not just move?" people in other places say, incredulous when they hear about the weather, the lack of jobs, or the frustrating inaccessibility of pad Thai. But you cannot leave a place where you are anchored by ghosts. Haunted by nostalgia and belonging. Land is so much more than a physical space, it's our spiritual center. We find significance in our sense of place. The way a New Yorker brags about the cost of a studio in Queens and the time he got punched on the subway, a Midwesterner brags about those two weeks the buses wouldn't run because it was colder here than it was in the Arctic. Our pain is our significance. Our survival is our belonging.

But as often as the brutality of space unites, it also isolates. I go back to the landscape, which seems expansive. A sweep of green stretching out to meet the unencumbered sky. The openness is a deception. I know that the places before me are filled with crops, commerce, fear, and expectation. The silence here is not an empty space, but one that is filled with expectations unsaid. And this is how values are imparted—not by what is spoken, but by what is hidden.

Middle America prides itself on close communities. And they are close and can be close, unless you don't belong. Moving to South Dakota as a teen and attending a public high school after being homeschooled for 14 years, with a Texan accent, a penchant for awkward hats, and an obsession with raising my hand in class to answer questions, I didn't belong. There was Carson who kicked me with his steel-toed boots when I answered a question in biology class. And then Dan who would ask me out very loudly in front of people and then say, "Oh right you can't because your parents made you take a virginity pledge."

I found friends, but we were all of a type—weird, gay, black, brown, vegans, witches, and homeschooled. But the lessons of who was in and who was out in church took longer to learn. In 1999, two women began attending the church in Vermillion, South Dakota, where my parents were members. I had been homeschooled and this was my first year of high school. I was struggling in math and chemistry, and one of the women offered to tutor me. Their house wasn't far from ours, and I biked over twice in the early fall of that year. At the kitchen table, one woman told me to view math as a mystery, each number and symbol a clue to a difficult answer. Like a detective, I had to look for the patterns, everything would be made clear. I remember the kitchen table was oak. I remember the house was red. And I remember that the lessons helped and the next time I biked over, the woman met me at the gate.

"Your mom wouldn't like it if you were here," she said. I balanced on my tiptoes, still straddling my bike, thinking of something to say.

"It's not you," she said. "It's just . . . we can't go to your church anymore."

When I came home, I asked my mom what was happening. She told me simply that the women were sinning. They had been asked not to sin and they refused. So, they were no longer welcome. I didn't ask any more questions. Anything else that was said was said in whispers or asides, passed around the bodies of children like a game of keep away. The women stopped coming. It wasn't until I was in college, when I went to dinner at a professor's house with some other students that I remembered. As she and her partner served us dishes of rice and chicken and filled our cups with sparkling water all around an oak table, I understood the cruelty of what had happened in my church.

Churches are supposed to be places of openness and community. But often, like the land, they isolate more than they unite. And the story of who leaves the church is just as important as the story of who stays. Churches in Middle America are struggling to find a place at the table for people. Millennials are labeled "religious nones," churches are segregated based on color, and queer people are often lost and cut out of community and support, especially in rural and empty spaces where they have nowhere to go.

Julie Rogers, a queer Christian and activist, tweeted, "Growing up in Texas and moving in evangelical spaces, I didn't know much anxiety I carried in my body. I wasn't aware of the depth of insecurity I felt in routine social interactions, always [self-conscious] about my clothes being too gay or my posture seeming too lezzy." Rogers explains that just living in a place where there are others like her, people who are visible, has given her a confidence and lightness of existence she didn't know was possible. Representation matters. Space matters. Who is in a church is just as important as who is outside of a church.

Years later, as an adult living in Iowa, I volunteered at a Wednesday night youth program at a church. A gay couple brought their sons. Every week, as they came down the hall to drop their sons off at the gym, the woman next to me would whisper, "It's the lesbians." This woman was older than me and a pastor's wife. A leader in the church. Her name was Gina, her husband was Adam. Later, they'd be the couple who convinced Dave and I to start a church with them. But now, we were just two women, volunteering on a Wednesday night with the youth.

"You need to stop doing that," I told her one week after the women left. "It's awkward and rude."

"Why do they even come here?" she said. "It's not like they believe in the Bible."

I would like to believe that I argued with her. I would like to believe that every time I have seen abuse and hate perpetuated in God's house, that I said something. But I know I must have instead answered with silence. My life and faith were held together by the silences I participated in just so I could belong.

In her book *Rescuing Jesus: How People of Color, Women, and Queer Christians Are Reclaiming Evangelicalism*, Deborah Jian Lee tells a similar story. As a young evangelical at the University of Illinois at Champaign-Urbana, Lee was involved in a group called InterVarsity. Yet, as she spoke about race and social justice to her friends, she was ostracized. She writes, "I loved my evangelical community and wanted to work through the issues. But as I expressed mostly liberal views, more and more evangelicals told me I was transgressing. One of my closest friends asked me, 'Are you even a

Christian anymore?' Like any human being, I was looking for a place where I belonged and was valued in my entirety, and I was no longer finding that in the evangelical world."[1] As a result, Lee found herself moving farther and farther away from the institutional church.

Lee's book is filled with stories of people of color, women, and queer Christians forced out of their churches because they spoke about race, voted Democrat, or dared to believe that their sexual orientation was not a mistake that needed to be rectified, but part of their beautiful and holy creation. It's hard to quantify these numbers. Churches don't collect data on the men and women who have been pushed out, either by outright rebuke or by whispers—rejection by a thousand staring eyes. Isolation by the complicity of silence. Frozen out by the mantra of "hate the sin and love the sinner" which only works if you aren't the sinner. And if the "sin" in question isn't a matter of choice but a matter of how you were created.

Christianity is losing adherents. There are a growing number of religious nones, who consider themselves spiritual but do not identify with a religion. According to the Pew Forum, they are now the third largest faith group in the Midwest. Driving the growth of this demographic shift are millennials; 35 percent of millennials identify as religious none and the numbers are growing. Of those identifying as religious none, 70 percent grew up in a religious tradition and 49 percent of them say they no longer identify with that tradition because they are "disenchanted" and "don't believe."[2]

The rise of the religious nones is often attributed to the consumer culture of millennials. I once sat through a sermon where a Baptist minister compared millennials choosing religion to someone shopping for a cell phone plan. Elizabeth Drescher, in her book *The Rise of the Nones*, makes that same connection between a sense of religious DIYness and consumer culture, albeit with a little more nuance, arguing that the increased pluralism of society and the variety of choice has influenced how people interact with their faith.

In his book *Shopping Malls and Other Sacred Spaces*, Jon Pahl argues that the consumer aspect of American Christianity is a kind of a feel-good cop-out of deeper truths. But for those who have been hurt by the church, who have been told their bodies are unacceptable in the eyes of God, or have witnessed other's pain perpetuated by religion, it is nothing of the sort. It's actually freedom. And it's freedom that has been sought and found by religious outsiders for millennia. The saints we revere like Joan of Arc and St. Francis of Assisi, were difficult nomadic outsiders who created their own religious spaces when none could be found for them. Even the model of Jesus, walking smelly and dirty in the desert with his band of fishermen, all men, was a rogue, cast out by the religious authorities. But these thoughts can be cold comfort when you are the one deemed unacceptable, deemed sinful by the very community that by its very precepts ought to love you.

Valerie, a queer poet, who also lives in Cedar Rapids, told me of her experience of growing up religious in a small town in Iowa, which she summarized as "I had to change or leave, because there wouldn't be room for me otherwise." She couldn't change her queerness. So she left to find a place where there was room for her. "There is no room at this table" is a constant message from churches resistant to change. This, coupled with struggling economies, means that the Midwest has the highest net losses of college-educated millennials than any other region in America.[3] We, the land of openness, the fields of opportunity, can be miserly with our bounty, fearful of change and difference.

* * *

Matt Anderson grew up in Columbus, Ohio. When I was looking for stories about faith in the Midwest, Matt leaped at the chance to talk to me. He was open and generous with his story, because he knew all too well it's the story of many people who are outside the church. Matt is gay and spent years hiding his sexuality from his family, friends, and church. He didn't have to be told he was unacceptable—not in so many words. But as he gradually revealed his self to his family by talking to them about boys he liked, they brushed it off. His parents would say, "Oh, you and him are just good friends."

At the age of fifteen, Matt finally came out to his parents. His mother's response was fine, but he described his father's reaction as "very bombastic, and very negative." "His initial response was just to not say anything," explained Matt. "And we didn't talk for two weeks. Then, after that, he just kind of laid into me about how wrong it is, how I'm going to hell—my life is going to be miserable."

His father's reaction created a tension for Matt. He began to believe that his gay identity and Christian identities could not coexist. After being sexually assaulted by another man when he was seventeen, Matt decided to embrace the Christian side of himself. He attended Taylor University, an

Evangelical college in Upland, Indiana. After his assault, Matt decided not to pursue his initial major in dance and instead focused on psychology. He would tell people that he wanted to become a pastor to inspire people with his story of overcoming his sexuality.

While he pursued his psychology degree, Matt had a professor explain to a class that homosexuality was a sexual disorder. The only cure was for gay men to have sex with women until their brain chemistry changed and they became straight. "I ended up walking out of that classroom, and I just didn't go back," said Matt. "It was too late in the semester to drop it, so I just took an F for that class. I was so angry and I think that's where I started to think that I couldn't reject this part of me anymore." Rejected by the church and by his college, Matt began again to grapple with his sexuality. He read *Washed and Waiting* by Wesley Hill, who argues that gay Christians are ordered to a life of celibacy. The book did little to encourage Matt: "It basically ends with [Hill] saying that he's lonely and sad, but still a good Christian."

And then Matt was assaulted again, this time at Taylor University. He had to get out. Matt moved to California for an internship at a church, but there he almost got fired because one of the parents of a student in the youth group suspected he might be gay after glancing at his Facebook profile.

There are a lot of LGBTQ-affirming churches in America; if he wanted to be a Christian, why didn't he go to one of them? His answer: "It's never that simple." For Matt, in Indiana, the "liberal" churches were the churches that had drums, preachers with beards and flannels—nondenominational churches that seem hip at the outset, but when you dig into their theology are actually very conservative. And while some mainline Protestant denominations were embracing queer Christians, Matt's Presbyterian church was one of a growing number threatening to break away from their denomination, based on their stance that gay people can be ministers.

And also, it isn't just about church, it is about community and family. It's hard to walk away from the place that raised you, the people who were there when you were baptized and promised to raise you in this holy family. The people who stood in the pews and prayed blessings over you. These are the people who bring you tater tot hot dish when your baby is one year old and you have a kidney infection. The people who remember to bring paper plates and lasagna to the hospital while you are there with your sister who was in a car accident. And they are the people who you most want to convince that you are worthy of loving—loving all of you, whether you are queer, Democrat, or a person of color. Losing a church is like losing a family. It's losing a foundation. Walking away for some is a slow leaving—a gradual sloughing of self. For others, it's a rip that leaves you bleeding, a wound that never fully heals.

Why did I stay in churches that I didn't like for so long? Why did any of us? Because we loved the people there, and we had been taught God was big enough for all of us, and we had the audacity to take those lessons at their word.

Matt did eventually leave the church, but it wasn't easy and with the absence of religion he tried so hard to find other ways to fit in. Even as he tried to reconcile his queerness with his Christianity, he embraced conservative politics so he'd fit in better with his church family. This of course alienated him from his gay friends, and as a result Matt found himself in a cycle of loneliness and isolation.

During this time, Matt discovered the Gay Christian Network, a website that offers resources and an online community for queer Christians. The acceptance and understanding he found online translated into his personal faith. He began to separate the religion of his childhood from his own personal faith.

Finally, he found space for his body.

Essays and articles passed among friends. Online discussion boards and Facebook groups, where covert communities of queers, feminists, and Christians of color gather and find solace—to Matt these replicate the early church in the New Testament, where gatherings were organic and happened in homes or in secret, for fear of persecution. This faithfulness is how Matt is able to call himself religious but without a church. How he is able to find God, without a minister. "It's not so much a part of being in an organized religion," explains Matt, "as it is emulating that faithfulness in your daily life."

Matt's acceptance of faith is one that was wrung hard from a life where the peace of Christian community has been hard to find. He's not pushing a shopping cart in a metaphorical mall of religion; he's struggling to come to terms with the understanding of his heart and the lived reality of his body. Deborah Jian Lee's work echoes this sentiment among queer Christians, women, and Christians of color throughout the Midwest, who like her have fought to find acceptance in communities of faith and instead found isolation. My own faith journey hasn't been much different. And even the church I helped to create isolated itself from me—establishing rules that separated me from structures of power and decision-making.

And yet, here I am again, now attending another church. A community where I have found comfort and acceptance. But in order to go there, I had to articulate my identity—as a woman, a feminist, an ally, and someone who desperately believes in the radical inclusion of all God's people at his table. And that articulation broke my marriage and relationships with friends and family. It's a wonder then, why anyone ever believes at all.

In the Heidelberg Disputation, Martin Luther writes, "Arrogance cannot be avoided nor can true hope be present, unless the judgement of damnation is feared in every work." What this means, Luther explains, is that hope in God is impossible "unless one has despaired regarding all creatures."

I know this means that hope in God cannot be full and complete without the knowledge that hoping in man is futile. But I think about that phrase "despaired regarding all creatures" and I think of my own feelings of separation while going to church. I think of the isolation I felt when I was begging my husband to go with me to an LGBTQ-affirming church. How, after all, can I participate in a faith if it's not for all people? How can I have a hope if it's not extended beyond the doors and borders of my heart? How can I say I despair without entering the despair of all people? How can I call a place a home, if it's not home for everyone?

My husband went with me once to the little liberal Lutheran church I had fallen in love with, and then he refused to go again. He told me a church that allowed gay people to lead violated his morals. When he told me that, I knew he believed himself to be the outcast, the moral rebel, the victim. In a religion founded on the broken body, we all feel ourselves to be martyrs. That's the verbal trick of this. We can all feel the victim. Jim, the friend from the broken church, had often preached sermons about the victimhood of white men in politically correct culture. He's not the only one. It doesn't take long to find communities of aggrieved men on Reddit or websites like Breitbart and Fox News. In a PRRI poll from late 2015, 57 percent of Republicans said they felt that white people were discriminated against.[4] The powerful are victims, the lowly oppressors. It's a topsy-turvy way of seeing a world, where power still rests in those white and male, who still hold more power in government, own more businesses, and outearn every other group of people.[5] It's hard to discern the lowly from the powerful when everyone is pointing a finger.

But I wonder if figuring out the difference is just a matter of how your power, no matter how limited, is used. Those true outcasts didn't close themselves off, but worked with what power they had to open up space for others even at the cost of their own bodies. It's Matt and Valerie eagerly sharing their stories in order that someone else feels less alone. It's Deborah Jian Lee faithfully opening up spaces with her words and work to allow others in. They too have despaired of all creatures and seen the damnation cast on them of others. It's a true hope.

Hope is a terrible endeavor. It's the triumph of will over experience. I think again of the immigrants who settled the Midwest: in Minnesota where pine needles drop away like prodigals from the upright trunks of their origins, or Nebraska, reaching to the sky like an open hand. In these places, they built again and again—after fire, insects, bitter winters, and such terrifying loss. We laud their tenacity, but even then, their legacy was built on blood-drenched soil. To find space requires a loss.

After Dave attends church with me and lectures me on its immorality, I decide to begin attending alone. That decision I knew was a break. And at first, he will not let my children come with me. So many Sundays I sit alone. The cleaving has begun, and I am both devastated and relieved. Pastor Ritva preaches about how even when we are empty, emptiness contains air and air is the breath of God. So our emptiness is God's breath—our despair is our very hope. I cry and feel like I am going to be okay. I'm only here in this place, trying again, but what I am building is also being built because there was first a loss.

7

A MUSCULAR JESUS

OUTSIDE THE STADIUM THERE IS A HEAVING FERVOR of bodies swathed in black and gold. Even in the early morning chill, the air smells of singed meat. People are drinking beer, liquor, wine, who knows what else, all in bottles, cans, and plastic cups. A woman underneath a black and gold canopy opens a package of hamburger buns, white and soft. Body and bread.

I am alone in the crowd, lost in the drunken religiosity of the University of Iowa tailgate. Women cheer. Men paint their bodies. There are babies. Entire families are here. Games of cornhole in between bleary-eyed college students. Black and gold awnings stretch out over pots of chili, sliders, bowls of cheese sauce, chips, Rice Krispy treats, and Special K bars. People want to give me food and be my friend. There are games of tippy cup and beer pong smooshed between cars. I'm wearing a University of Iowa shirt I borrowed from a friend. "Go Hawks!" a girl with blonde hair screams. She has University of Iowa temporary tattoos on her cheeks. She is so tan and beautiful. The men she's with have thick necks and strong chins. Young bodies already heavy from beer.

For several years, the University of Iowa has ranked in the top five for party schools according to the *Princeton Review*. Recently it's fallen to number six, but it's hard to tell from the throngs of bodies dipping and swaying to a ponderous beat, blue cans of Budweiser already crushed on the ground by 7:00 a.m. Most of the people here won't even go inside the stadium to see the game. So, they will sit and watch on TV or listen on radios, phones, or computers. Or go into a bar and watch among a communion of strangers. The hue and cry a perfect chorus, when points are tallied and bodies are broken.

The stadium sits at the center of it all—a temple to a weekend god of flesh.

There are no official statistics to tell me how many people are here tailgating. Harder still to quantify the people at home, watching the game from the comfort of their couches. But numbers couldn't quite capture the way college football is part of the culture of this place. When I moved to Iowa, people kept asking me if I was an Iowa or Iowa State fan. It was part of the cultural currency, a way to establish a common bond. When I'd say I was agnostic, conversations quickly dried up. At my gym, at parties, wherever people meet, sports become a commonality on which we can build our relationships. While giving birth to my second child, the anesthesiologist who showed up to give me the epidural was wearing an Iowa State lanyard; the nurses teased him for being a State fan in Hawkeye territory. I sat between them, partially undressed and in pain. I coughed in irritation.

The doctor looked down at me. "Who do you cheer for?"

"Whoever gets this epidural in me," I said.

A few minutes later, drugs coursing through my body, the doctor asked me how I felt. I said, "Like an Iowa State fan." The next day, he sent my infant son a gift of a tiny hat in Iowa State colors.

At the tailgate, in borrowed Iowa colors, I feel like a stranger in this place. I've never once tailgated despite living here for twelve years. I know this town though, I come here often. And yet, the places I frequent are not the same ones I'm visiting today. I've never been to the stadium. I've never been to the bar where I'll go drink a beer before slinking off home before the game even starts. It's not that I don't know how to be in this space—I could have come with friends after all. I could have been very drunk; I am very good at beer pong, or at least that's how I remember it from college.

But it feels empty to participate in a ritual you don't believe in. Don't get me wrong, I want to belong here. I want to scream "woo," then go and apply lipstick in a bathroom, woozy from liquor, beads clanking in the stall behind me. I want to lounge in a chair and laugh loudly with my friends and ask about the future of the team and discuss the running back's latest injuries. I know how to do it. I've grown up sitting next to men, watching them as they watch other men shove a cylindrical object across an arbitrary line. In college, I was good at it too. Eating wings, drinking beer, but not too much to wreck the lines of my body. Knowing just enough so that I could join the conversation, but never enough so that I was an expert. I knew enough of the starting lineup and who was good and who wasn't, so that I could say benign things when necessary or shout out a player's name in frustration. I've worn low-slung jeans and cropped shirts and sidled up next to men with baskets of wings as they reach for my thigh under the table, eyes never leaving the TV screen.

Part of me wants to do this now. I know that game. I know there is acceptance in it. I wish I had chosen to come with my friends—to get swept away in all of this ritual. If I had, I'd at least feel like I belong, like I was part of something bigger than myself.

But these ritual sports potlucks—these beery communions—they are not full participation. I have to remind myself. This isn't a world that allows me to fully participate. Women are a growing market for the NFL, as evidenced by the preponderance of feminine-cut jerseys and sportswear. And I have many female friends who are smarter about the sport than their male peers. Yet our bodies are not allowed to play. It is not us on the field being broken. That is not my skin in this game. Commercials show women sexily sipping shitty beer next to men mesmerized by a screen.

In this religion, my role is on the sidelines, cheering.

* * *

Growing up in Texas, my father called Dallas Cowboy's games "religious programming." It was the only television we were allowed for many years. Commercials muted so the advertisements with their innuendo wouldn't spoil our minds. But the flesh was there anyway, already gleaming on the television. The sweat-buffed luster of black, white, and brown skin, tight clad in pads and helmets. The game is a sacrifice of sons. Their bodies and brains, knocked about for the sin of our amusement.

Born in the colleges of the East Coast during the late 1800s, football evolved as a hybrid form of rugby and soccer. It quickly found popularity in the frozen fields of the Midwest—starting in Michigan, then spreading to Illinois, Minnesota, and Kansas. The violence of the game must have appealed on an intuitive level to scrappy Americans, used to clawing their existence out of nothing. Planting blood into the field like the parable of the sower, who tossed seeds onto the earth.

And those seeds found fertile soil, because Americans love nothing more than sacrificing their sons for sport. So the game evolved and found a footing in the hard scrabble hearts of boys in rural areas—farms in the Midwest and the South, where the violence of raw masculinity is heralded as a savior for whatever ails us.

There is an apocryphal story from the early days of American football: a Rutgers professor cycled up to watch students play a pick-up game of football. After watching for a while, he shook his fist at them and yelled, "You lot will come to no Christian end!"

This game is at odds with American Christianity.

* * *

Every pastor I ask in my research tells me that sports are the biggest challenge to their ministry. Families take their kids to practice after school and on Wednesday nights—a night traditionally reserved for youth group. Some school districts still honor the policies of no Wednesday night games or practices, but in places where there is little else to do and schools—and churches too—have been consolidated, the games continue. And the families aren't fighting it. They want it. They sign their kids up. They lament of course about the cost and the stress. But they still do it. Sports. Teamwork. Lessons for life. I don't even like sports, but I still put my kids in soccer, then tennis, then whatever else they ask for. Maybe I want them to fit in better than I do.

And so, there are practices on Wednesday and games on Sundays. Games on Saturdays. Games and practice early Friday morning. "When I was raising kids, we didn't enroll our kids in all those activities," laments Evelyn Birkby. Other pastors tell me this too—some old, but a lot are young. Hunting season interferes as well. So do fishing openers, but sports is the thing that pastors see as cutting into their diminishing communities.

I meet Joella as I'm picking at my ham salad sandwich at a drug store in Sydney, Iowa. The food is flesh colored. I ordered it because it's ham salad, the food of the region. I'm in a town that balances on the Iowa edge of the Iowa-Nebraska border. Of all the choices—turkey, ham, ham salad, or liverwurst—I thought ham salad was the safest. This is the land of ham salad after all. But it was a bad choice. I can't taste any dill pickles in there and the mayo is Miracle Whip, which is an affront to mayo.

The bread on the sandwich is good—the soft, cheap smooshy kind that I'm sure they just got from Fairway. But the ham salad has the same consistency. The only buffer is the crunch of iceberg lettuce. I'm hungry. I haven't had anything since five in the morning, when I stopped for gas and a slice of breakfast pizza at a Casey's.

So I eat small bites of sandwich and hunch forward, listening to Evelyn tell me about her town. How it used to be, how it is now. She misses the community. She tells me this as she takes small bites of her liverwurst sandwich. Women walk in and greet her, ask about her health. Evelyn introduces me as a writer, but she pats my hand, vouching for me.

Joella is one of these women, and she sits down and tells me about her church, a beautiful Catholic church just up in the next town over. It's a drive that she hates to make in the snow, so they don't get out there much in the winter and then in the summer their grandkids have sports.

I ask her where people find community now that it's not in churches. She gives me that look that implies I've just asked a dumb question. "Sports, honey," she tells me patiently like I'm a toddler. "Our schools are closing, our churches are closing. We have craft fairs and our libraries are good at hosting get-togethers for people like me who like to quilt or some of the young girls are taking up cross-stitch, but it's sports."

It's sports that gives so many of these communities structure and meaning. Sports as activity. Sports as religion. Sports as a shared language. A shared narrative. If you can't talk to your neighbor about anything, talk to him about the Cubs or better yet, Iowa State. We are so close to Nebraska, so there are a lot of Corn Husker fans here too.

Around sports there is communal food—bean salads, ham and Swiss sliders (my favorite, on King's Hawaiian rolls, doused in butter and baked until the bottoms are crisp). There are chicken wings and dips—cheesy dips, sour cream–based dips, guacamole. I love a cheesy artichoke dip. But there is also a chicken wing dip—made of cream cheese, wing sauce, and chicken bits—that tastes like a beautiful heart attack. So many foods that whenever I eat of them and so many beers that when I drink of them, I remember the reason for their existence. Sports. Always sports.

So, I make a pilgrimage to one of the temples—Kinnick Stadium. I go alone because, even though friends have offered to take me, I want to be able to leave whenever I want to. It's overwhelming. Especially as the day rolls on and the crowds grow. The sticky yeast smell of beer connects everything. Students chug suspicious-looking liquids from water bottles. I was in a sorority, so I'm not unfamiliar with what is inside. Probably vodka, Gatorade, or maybe just whatever was left over from the puerile stew created in a cooler the night before—a stone soup of liquors. We called it "Jungle Juice"—but that was a long time ago. I don't know what these kids call it. And who knows what my kids will call it. Whatever it is, it's the reason I don't like Bacardi anymore.

I didn't go to a school with a Division 1 football team, and I only attended football games when it was a mandatory sorority sisterhood activity. But even here, walking like a stranger through the crowds, I can feel a pull of nostalgia. There is something here of a return, of a connection, to something, I'm not sure what. For me, it might be when I could wear a crop top and not care. But there is something else here—it's a return, a constant circling back to a pattern, a ritual.

I hear people sing a fight song. Everyone around me joins in.

This is liturgy.

* * *

When I was fourteen, my father joined Promise Keepers, a movement begun by Bill McCartney, a former football player and coach for the University of Colorado at Boulder. McCartney's mission, as he saw it, was to imbue American men with a sense of masculine purpose and faith. They were to rejoin their churches and their communities and take charge. They met in football stadiums and listened to speaker after speaker encourage a muscular Christianity. One that eschewed intellectualism and the effeminate encroachment that was threatening their God-given roles. The signs were everywhere, I heard more than one pastor argue—the rise of single-mom households, the overwhelming number of female volunteers in churches.

Promise Keepers was founded in 1990, the same decade that saw professional football explode in popularity. The NBA and the NHL faced strikes and lockouts, while the NFL expanded. By the early 2000s, football, more than any other sport, became America's game.

The rise of Promise Keepers closely mirrors the rise of football in America. While the materialism and conspicuous consumption dominated the narrative of the 1980s, Middle America was in a crisis. The farm crisis decimated family farms—resulting in crippling debt and suicide. Land and lives were lost. It was an emasculating time. "A man doesn't feel like a man if he can't feed his family," said Steve W., a farm credit officer I spoke to in Illinois. He was just a kid then, but he still sees the effects now in the fears of farmers, struggling to hold onto their land. "It's not just land, its identity," he said. "It's who these men are."

It makes sense that Americans would find another way of asserting this masculinity now at risk. A new religion. One of muscle and blood. A different kind of hope and a different kind of Jesus—one enmeshed in the sweat and violence of skin and sphere. There is meaning here, and the men of the heartland still hold onto it. Clutching it in sweating cans of watery beer, fingers greasy with remnants of chips. Body and blood. Bread and wine.

Sports and religion have long shared a narrative. The ancient Olympic Games were created as an act of worship to the gods. Religion teaches us that our bodies are god-inspired, therefore what we do with them, how we move them, is an extension of the divine. The apostle Paul used sports metaphors in his writing. "Let us run the race with patience," he exhorted early Christians, "the race that is set before us." His words also tell Christians that their bodies are temples of the Holy Spirit—a passage of the Bible frequently used to encourage Christians to exercise and eat healthy food.

If your body is a temple, then your muscles, your sinew, your very bones, are claimed by God. In the Old Testament, the prophet Daniel, while living as a prisoner in exile, abstained from the rich food of the palace, eating instead only vegetables and drinking only water. Eventually, as the king notices, Daniel and his friends "seemed better and they were fatter than all the youths who had been eating the king's choice food."

Athleticism is morality. Rousseau codified this idea in *Emile*, and the English preacher Charles Kingsley made it popular with his novel *Two Years Ago*. The idea has spread since then and woven itself into the fabric of sports, the YMCA, the FCA; no one in American blinks an eye if a professional athlete pauses in the end zone to kneel and offer a prayer to the Christian God.

But the tangle of sports and religion isn't just about bodies and how they are expressed, but about one specific kind of body—the male body. A heterosexual male's sense of body. Because this is the same strain of Christianity that suppresses the female body—covering it up with verses about modesty. John Piper, former head pastor of the Midwestern megachurch Bethlehem Baptist and founder of the Center for Biblical Manhood and Womanhood, once preached, "God revealed Himself in the Bible pervasively as king not queen; father not mother. . . . Second person of the Trinity is revealed as the eternal Son not daughter; the Father and the Son create man and woman in His image and give them the name man, the name of the male."[1]

Christianity is masculine, Piper concludes.

As a result, the body that is uplifted in this religion is male. The experience that is centered is heterosexual and white. All other bodies deemed deviant are ignored, erased, or condemned. Pictures of Jesus defiantly depict a Middle Eastern man as white. Countless pastors in sermons preached throughout my life will tell me that my body leads men to sin. I will see gay women and men pushed out of their faith communities. But it won't occur to me how white this conception of faith is until I attend a faith conference made by and for people of color.

There, surrounded by bodies so different from my own, I will encounter a fleshy Christianity of a different kind. One that values, not erases, deviant bodies. That sees them as divine. At this conference, I will attend a spiritual workshop taught by a black woman, the aim of which is to liberate the body. I will move, I will bend, sing, and shout, and I will be moved to tears when the woman leading the workshop tells me that my body is a part of worship too. Holding back and hiding it is selfish, she will chide. Give it up to the creator. And I will, feeling happy and free and also very sad, because I could have been living like this for so long.

But right now, I am in Iowa City, here to worship the body of a muscular Jesus being martyred for yet another touchdown.

This is the faith of the tailgate.

This hyper masculinity comes at a cost. In 1979, University of Iowa's head coach, Hayden Fry, had the locker room of the opposing team painted pink. In his memoir, he wrote he did this because pink "is often found in girls' bedrooms, and because of that some consider it a sissy color." Fry goes on to brag, "I can't recall a coach who has stirred up a fuss about the color and then beaten us."

The locker room is still pink. Every once in a while, a well-meaning university professor will point out the toxic nature of the gesture as one that denigrates the traditionally feminine. In 2014, communications studies professor Kembrew McLeod wrote in an op-ed for the *Iowa City Press Citizen*, "Does a pink locker room directly lead to violence against women and gay people? Of course not, but it does reinforce the narratives about what it means to be a 'real' man that kids are exposed to from a very young age."[2]

But the op-eds and protests never work. The professors get death threats. The university administrators argue that pink has a "calming effect," as if we believe that. But there is a lot of money in this toxic display of masculinity, so it remains. Another marker of what is deemed acceptable and what isn't.

* * *

Exclusion is also a hallmark of American Evangelicalism. In 1990, the pastor of a large church in California told a reporter, "The contemporary perspective is that church isn't for the weak, infirm, unintelligent. It's relevant to the young, active mover-shaker. . . . That means more of a 'one-stop, supermarket approach' to spirituality. . . . People expect spick-and-span nurseries, drug and alcohol counseling, even Monday Night Football events."

There are no weak and no infirm and they are all led by men. A 1998 study found that only 2 percent of Evangelical congregations are led by women.[3] This is a number unlikely to be much different even a decade later, owing to orthodox religious beliefs that hold that women should not be lead pastors. And in all of Christian religions, female ministers only make up 10 percent of head pastors.[4] My faith life, like my sports life, has been one of observance rather than participation.

I feel that here too in this tailgate. Who made this food? Who packed these coolers? Who purchased these groceries? Who is watching the children of these men? But this is not what we celebrate in the early chill with beer, beads, face paint, chants, and ill-conceived concoctions of booze. We are here to cheer on the male body—muscle and might. Body and blood broken and shared for you. Here we gather in these temples on these grounds, offering burnt offerings to those we worship—men—allowing them to consume the first fruits of our labors. Our faith is in American maleness—of its glory and triumph and ability to save America if only it would charge forth and convert those yards into touchdowns. Play a little defense once in a while.

Pastors of these small churches believe that sports are competing with faith. But that's not exactly the case. Sports are changing faith to be sure, but the people here believe in God. They love Jesus. This is evident from the prayers, the righteous elevation of one nation "under God." The problem is not belief, but the worship at a temple that reifies heteronormative male narratives about who God is, at the cost of the rest of us, silenced and ignored, forced to stand on the sidelines of a faith we are told is not for us.

And too, what of the men we sacrifice up there on those brutal crosses? A trainer at my gym played football for the University of Iowa. At the age of twenty-five, he's had seven knee surgeries. "It's not the age, it's the mileage," he's fond of saying as he grimaces and stretches his broken body. Sports are second only to motor vehicle crashes as the leading cause of traumatic brain injury among high school and college-aged students.

It's no accident that the pastor of the Evangelical church attended by my now ex-husband is a former college football player. Many of his sermons are peppered with sports analogies and anecdotes about his own career. He often mocks femininity as "too emotional"—using gender as a punch line. He's popular, everyone likes him. He's affable and a great public speaker.

And again, I wanted to fit in there. Everyone in the church is kind, well-dressed, they look and talk like some sort of variation of Chip and Joanna

Gaines. The church even has reclaimed barn wood on the walls. They'd have shiplap too if this was a house instead of a renovated warehouse. I want to squeeze myself into this role assigned to me—doting wife, good mother, worshipper of the male voice, the male god, the muscular Jesus, that requires I only work in the children's ministry, or go to women's Bible studies.

And what does that matter anyway? I don't want to be a pastor, do I? Why can't I just fit in? Why can't I just make it work? And I had for many years. My whole life. I know the moves and the language. I know how to brush my hair, wear my earrings, which books to read, and when to stay silent. I've spent my whole life doing it, believing that this was the cost of my life. The sacrifice of faith was to constantly feel the blisters of this ill-fitting religion. So why now?

But the church is not a tailgate. The cost of not joining in the church is my marriage. It's my friendships. It's the stability and the life that I've worked so hard to build. I know that. I knew that, even in the beginning when the ultimatums were unspoken.

Walking through the tailgate, I feel every bit of the outcast I believe myself to be. I have to remind myself, I've chosen this split. I've chosen to come to this place alone. And I chose to walk out of that church with its football pastor and muscular faith. The reason being simply that I no longer believe.

The next morning, I go to church, my church—the liberal Lutheran congregation that I've made my home in the days since my marriage collapsed. One pastor is gay. One pastor is female. The sermons contain lines from poems and children are allowed to run free in the sanctuary. During communion my friend assures me that I can in fact bring my four-year old and six-year old up to the table. I do, and I watch as the pastor offers my children bread and juice. Body and blood. My daughter smiles and asks for more of that "good bread." She's given it and I cry.

My son grabs the small cup with wine in it instead of the juice. I'm not used to having wine at communion, so I don't register the error until I see him slamming it down—holding the empty communion cup in his chubby fists. I'm horrified, but I also have to hold my breath to keep from laughing too loudly.

These are small revelations. But here, faith feels like a comfort rather than a violence. And this is why sports is hurting American churches—not through competition for attention but through the pernicious marketing of a narrative that has nothing to do with Jesus.

8

THE ASIAN AMERICAN REFORMED
CHURCH OF BIGELOW, MINNESOTA

Bigelow, Minnesota, has a population of 235, but every Sunday
the town doubles in size. Positioned on the border of Iowa and Minnesota, the town is only a few blocks with a small main street. Businesses
and homes and a grain elevator—wide open lawns blend into one another.
There are very few fences and the town smells like damp earth and freshly
cut grass from Saturday's mowing. The drive to Bigelow is the kind of drive
I enjoy—open highways, pink dawn, and the warm damp surge of highway
air through my windows.

This is a manufacturing town. Many of the people here work in
Worthington, which is just a few miles away. Housing is cheaper here, with
the median home value at $86,268 compared to Worthington's $134,269.
A little over 6 percent of the population have a college degree, 40 percent
work in manufacturing, and 80 percent are white.[1]

When I arrive on a warm summer morning, I have a hard time finding
a space to park. Not because there are a lot of cars, but because there are no
parking lots. The town is just road and grass.

I've arrived early for worship at the Asian American Reformed
Church of Bigelow. There are three services, which occur in five different
languages—Karen, Lao, English, Vietnamese, and Spanish; I'm there for
the one that will be held in English and Vietnamese. No one is around when
I pull behind the church, opting to park in the grassy yard rather than the
road. I don't want to block off a neighbor's driveway on accident. And even
though I don't see anyone, I feel seen.

It's impossible to drive into a town like this and not be noticed.

Pastor Ron, who oversees the Asian American Reformed Church, estimates that around three hundred people cycle through the church every

Sunday. This feat is a resurrection for the little church, which was once declared "dead" by the Christian Reformed Church in America and cut off from any denominational support.

The church was founded in 1913 by eight families. They met in homes and then later had services at the public school. On June 15, 1915, the church became an official member of the Christian Reformed Church of America, with thirty-five baptized members. The church building was completed in 1919. It's a little white church with modest lancet-style stained-glass windows. The church has been added onto, with a sloping entryway in the front that dips off the front of the building like a broken nose. The church is just on the edge of town and the world behind it stretches out into farmland. For fifteen years, the services were held entirely in Dutch. They added English services in 1928. What I am saying is, this church was white. The kind of Dutch Caucasian white that is a charming staple of the Midwest. The town still has this feel, with the close-cut lawns and clean shabby houses, fading, but well loved. The whole time I'm there, I don't see any litter on the ground.

The families who founded the church all have names that show their Dutch roots—Vander Plaats, Dykstra, Van Reenen. Shirley is a member of the church and has lived her whole life in Nobels County. She still remembers Dutch being spoken in the church service. Inside, the church is plain and clean. Wooden pews and homemade curtains.

The church was never that big, with twenty-two families in 1964 and never growing much beyond that. The town was hit hard by the farm crisis of the 1980s, and they lost what Shirley estimates to be about half the congregation. The congregation had barely been holding on before that—not much money and very few people. In 1965, they considered disbanding, but ultimately voted against it. There was, and still is, a Reformed church in Worthington, just three miles away and it has always made sense, from a denominational standpoint, to just consolidate. And the pressure from the denomination to close only increased as the church struggled.

But people don't survive here because they quit easily. It's the summer, so the land looks green and generous, but this is not a place that gives up its bounty easily. You don't squeeze a living from this miserly dirt only to close up because some suits who never visit told you to do so. In fact, that only makes you want to hang on tighter.

"We're stubborn," Shirley tells me. She and her husband, Dennis, have a dairy farm. They invited me over to their house after church to talk about the congregation and its history. Their house is vintage modern—with the gleaming oak paneling and sharp corners that define houses built in the mid-1970s. Every inch is filled with paper and knick-knacks—the comfortable calamity of a life of saving. Shirley and Dennis, like everyone here, have a hard time letting go.

They serve me iced coffee purchased from the store, mixed with cream straight from their cows. It's so rich it feels like a meal. The cream coats my tongue like a velvet dress. As we talk, a fly buzzes in the house and Dennis asks her to swat it. Shirley rolls her eyes. "It's part of the family now." I see what she means by stubborn.

When Ron was hired as a pastor in 1977, the church had only nineteen families. And in 1984, the only other church in town, the Methodist Church, closed. In the wake of the Vietnam War, immigrants from Laos and Vietnam began to arrive in the Midwest. Iowa's governor at the time, Robert Ray, welcomed refugees from the Vietnam War with open arms, resettling 1,400 Tai Dam, an ethnic minority from northwest Vietnam, and pledging to accept 1,500 more refugees.

By the late 1980s, a couple of the Laotian families in town were attending the church, but it wasn't enough to instill faith in the denomination. In 1990, after a long fight, Pastor Ron convinced the denomination to keep the church open. But there was a catch: they were no longer a full church but a "Mission," whose sole purpose was outreach to the Asian immigrants in the area. On June 24, 1990, one week after celebrating their seventy-fifth anniversary, the church held its last English service.

"The congregation had been warned," explained Shirley. "If they wanted to go to another church, they could. So, most of them did. We come to church next Sunday and the white people were essentially gone."

Only three white families remained. When Shirley walked into the church that Sunday morning, the place was almost empty. She sat down in a pew and cried. One of the Laotian women, Grace, hugged Shirley and reassured her that things would be all right and that God had a plan. "The next week," Shirley said, "we had so many people, I never had a moment to cry since." The church was flooded with Vietnamese families. Very few spoke English and only a few actually lived in Bigelow, but they were there to worship.

Shirley and Dennis stayed at the church because Dennis had been attending the church since 1941 and he wasn't about to change. And Shirley explained simply, "God brought us there and He brought them to us." So they remained, even as they felt apprehensive about the changes. Dennis fought in Vietnam, and Shirley was worried about him at the time. Dennis grimaced when Shirley told me this. I asked what she meant and she explained that it might bring some stuff up for him—stuff he didn't want to deal with.

Dennis was silent. I looked at him, but he just shrugged his shoulders. There is a lot in that silence. Unspoken resentments. Loss. Death. Fear. The wounds of history still fresh and bleeding there in the pews of that small church. Everything is political. Our wounds and our worship. We want our faith to transcend the political, but we can only do that when we exist in sameness. When barriers collapse, our wounds are revealed, and wounds are political because they involve pain. For a moment, no one says anything. In that silence, history marches through the room. Finally, I ask, "How is it now?"

"Oh," says Shirley, "They just hug him."

I don't for a second believe that the pains of war for Dennis or for those in the church can be solved with a hug—or several hugs for that matter. But I don't think anyone is claiming to have solved a problem—they've only committed to living together, for all the trauma and grace that means.

* * *

After the last Sunday as a Reformed church, everything changed. They became their own entity and began to grow. The church added two new pastors: Pastor Tran and Pastor Dedthanou.

One of the white members who remained drove a bus that would shuttle people between Worthington and Bigelow, but it still wasn't enough. In 1997, the denomination issued a report that told the church to move to Worthington, promising to end support for Ron. In the booklet that describes the hundred-year history of the church, the small note on those events is brief but telling: "The report was not received with much satisfaction."

Shirley told me it was around this time that she phoned the Missions Office and demanded that the denomination send someone to the church to see the work they'd been doing. The call didn't go well, and Shirley was vague on the specifics, insisting she didn't remember. But she did tell me she ended the call by shouting, "You might be the Missions Office, but you aren't God!"

After the report, Pastor Tran moved and eventually so did Pastor Dedthanou. But even without the support of the denomination, the families kept coming and the church stayed open. Pastor Ron began to learn Thai, Lao, and Karen and recruited members of the church to preach. The denomination agreed to continue to support Pastor Ron by designating him a missionary, but that solution didn't last long and in 2002 Ron officially retired and began to draw on his pension.

He isn't retired at all. The Sunday I visited the church, he, with the help of Pastor Somsanuk Souksawan, held the service in Lao. After the service, we went downstairs for a potluck, as the Spanish service began. That group is led by Guatemalan missionaries; they had been meeting in homes in Worthington but needed to find a place with more parking.

"There are twenty-six churches in Worthington," Shirley told me. "And all they [the Guatemalan missionaries] wanted was a place to meet, they'd adjust to anyone's schedule just so they could have a place to worship." Pastor Ron heard about the request on a church listserv, and according to Shirley he said, "This is God's church for Heaven's sake! And we don't use it after 11 a.m." Pastor Ron just says he saw an ad and reached out. "Shirley will tell you the story," he told me when I asked. And Shirley tells me everything.

The relationship began awkwardly. Pastor Ron thought they might be a cult and for their part, the Guatemalan group didn't know what to make of this white man and his church of Laotians and Karen. In the first few weeks that the Guatemalan's worshipped in the building, they didn't bring their children. Shirley noticed and figured they were wary of the white strangers running the church. After several weeks, couples began bringing their children, and when I peeked into the service, the aisle was lined with baby carriers. I wasn't allowed to go in, though. The church is very conservative, and men and women do not sit on the same side. All of the women wore head coverings and dresses—I was wearing pants.

The music from the Guatemalan service thumped over our heads, while I made halting conversation over plates of sticky rice, kaipen, tam mak hoong, ping gai, and nam van. Many of the members of the church don't speak English, and the potluck was segregated, white people at one side, Laotians on the other, but everyone sharing the same food. The conversation was genial but halting. Everyone was very concerned that I avoid the spicy food, which just made me want to try it more. A Laotian woman, noticing tam mak hoong on my plate, brought me an extra bowl of sticky rice.

I was fine. I'd spent thirteen years of my life attending potlucks in church parking lots in Texas, where the heat swirled off the cement, and when the grownups weren't looking us kids dared each other to eat jalapenos whole, with glasses of milk at the ready.

The food of the church is one of its most powerful languages, communicating culture and values with the heat and sweet of the dishes that crowd around the long tables. When my family first moved from Texas to South Dakota, my mother got into trouble by putting the Jell-O salad on the dessert table. An older woman silently moved it back to the table with the salads. My mom moved it over to the dessert table. They did this, back and forth, the older woman never saying a word and my mom, getting increasingly frustrated, until a kind woman took my mom aside.

"Jell-O is a salad," she explained.

My mom laughed. "It's got marshmallows!"

"But also fruit," the woman said seriously.

I am told the Guatemalan and the Karen churches each have their own potlucks. I wonder what the original potlucks were like, when the Dutch immigrants gathered here to worship God in their language—finding a brief respite in the community, the shared language, and all the food. Was there cheese and ontbijtkoek? Fish and bitterballen?

I think of all the potlucks I've been too—places with soup and sandwiches, large piles of fried chicken and homemade biscuits. Ham and tater tot casserole. Wilting kale salad. And glistening Jell-O salad. Tamales. Cheesy potatoes. And now, here in Bigelow, Minnesota, there are plates of rice and spicy papaya.

This isn't the Minnesota I know. But it is still Minnesota. The Reverend Martin Luther King Jr., once said "that the most segregated hour of Christian America is eleven o'clock on Sunday morning."[2] This still holds true. Only 14 percent of American congregations qualify as multiracial, and most of these congregations exist in larger urban areas.[3]

Martin Luther King Jr. believed this segregation was appalling— evidence that America had done little to address the systemic racial problems that plague our nation. And it is. Existing in white sameness allows us to forget we are oppressing. To believe lies like, "Oh, I'm not political, just a Christian."

But this Sunday segregation for people of color often offers a coda of relief to a week of nothing but assimilation. My friend Kathy, the daughter of Korean immigrants, tells me that for people of color, Sunday segregation isn't a problem, it's a blessing. She tells me how her life as a woman of color in America is all about fitting into spaces not designed for her in a white

Christian world, but Sunday is her one day to belong. She tells me it's the only time her parents get to speak their language.

My friend Paly, a Muslim who grew up in London, tells me the same thing. She was never very religious until she moved to Cedar Rapids, Iowa. Now she sends her children to Sunday school at the mosque every week and is an active member of her religious community because it's one of the few places she can find that she belongs without question and without threat.

Americans love to fetishize the melting pot, as if in the crucible of our country we all somehow meld as one. But what we really mean by melting pot is that everyone becomes like us—white and Christian. When I had been told to go to Bigelow by a seminarian, I was told it was almost a utopia—the perfect version of God's mission here on earth. This was going to be how the rural church survives, he told me—by embracing our brothers and sisters from different cultures.

It wasn't quite that easy. It never is. It was clear Pastor Ron was the only one of the white congregants who had bothered to learn any other language. And the Laotian congregants were here for community, to speak their own language, to find a moment of verbal rest in a place where they are the minority. Here they are not the ones struggling with conversation over meals they don't understand.

And the situation is less than utopian. During Pastor Ron's sermon, there were mentions of the "false idols" that the Laotians used to worship. He demeaned traditional Laotian practices as Devil worship, in a language that smacked of a colonial condemnation. What's preached here is an expectation to assimilate. It's a welcoming imperialism, but still imperialism.

The relationship between the church and the town hasn't been easy either. Most of the people in the church live in Worthington, few actually live in town. And the ones that do have faced cultural isolation and misunderstandings. Shirley told me a story of a Laotian couple who got married without a civil ceremony. The husband paid the bride-price to the father-in-law and the couple moved in together. But the young bride, K, was still in high school and was only seventeen. People started to talk. Eventually, social services came to the house and took K away. Community leaders in nearby Sioux City tried to intervene, but while the situation was being sorted out, K was in foster care and no one knew where she was.

Shirley tells me that was when she stepped in. She knew people, so she put the word out in the county. Her sister-in-law knew someone at a vet's office, who knew where K was. K moved in with Shirley and Dennis for a short time, and they let her husband visit her. There was also a contract written in Laotian between the father and the husband. Shirley had signed it and eventually took a copy to the police so they wouldn't press charges. Shirley didn't like the sheriff, but she knew him in the way people know people in small places. She knew he'd been kicked out of little league games for yelling at the umpire, and she knew he was difficult. She gave him a copy of the contract and told him to back off, which he eventually did. But the resentments run deep. "I better not meet him in a dark alley," Shirley told me. "It won't go well for either of us." K eventually moved back in with her husband, but the two separated not long after. She remarried and lives in Worthington.

When I asked Shirley and Dennis why they fought so hard for K, Shirley tells me with her Midwestern humility that she was simply doing what any neighbor would do. "These are our friends. They are our faith family."

Her words make me well up with tears. This is faith in action, I believe. But my feelings of hope don't last long. I get into my car and listen to the news, which is full of the controversy about President Donald Trump's Muslim ban. Shirley and Dennis don't want to talk politics. I can't blame them; America is tense and they don't know me. But this town voted overwhelmingly for Donald Trump in the 2016 election—a president who objects to the immigration practices and policies that have given life to this area of the Midwest. The same policies that allowed this church to survive.

How do the two meet? How does a mission of outreach and support to immigrant communities square with the repressive politics of the region? In a way, it's the guiding question of this book—how can a nation that professes to be majority Christian become a breeding ground for hate? How can Evangelical leaders like Franklin Graham preach purity for women from the pulpit and still support as president a man who brags about grabbing women by the pussy? How can people who have seen me spend my whole life struggling to live and practice my faith call me godless?

How can a message of peace and unity bring so much pain and loss and destruction?

When I ask what is happening to our churches, what I really want to know is what is happening to our souls?

I ask Pastor Ron about the way the town voted and what it says about their attitude toward the immigrant community they support. I expect him to tell me something about abortion or something about the character of rural America, but instead he shakes his head. "The Democrats should have run someone better than that woman."

That woman.

It appears it was never about faith after all. Instead, it's always been about power.

My friend Paly helps me understand this. She tells me how often she is friends with people, invites them into her home, has coffee with them, only to see them post anti-Muslim rhetoric on social media. "They know me, I am their friend, I am not a threat," she says. "But it was never about friendship or goodness. It's about power. They don't want to change."

Oscar Wilde writes in *The Soul of Man under Socialism*, "It is much more easy to have sympathy with suffering than with thought."[4] This is easy to see in the kindness of Bigelow and the charity practiced by churches across the Midwest. It's the logic that says, "My friend who is Muslim is okay, but not those other Muslims out there." It is an ideology that asserts, "These immigrants are good, while the others are bad."

* * *

I hear a pastor, the one at the church I will never go to again, preaching from the pulpit on a Sunday right before the 2016 election. "Jesus wasn't political," he said. "So don't look for politics to save you." The line brought cheers and applause from the majority white, upper-middle-class audience. It's a miserly faith that offers heaven but denies the voting booth—a faith that cries out for freedom in God, but denies freedom to all.

The response to suffering in a Christian context is charity and kindness. But Slavoj Žižek argues that charity is the wrong response, noting, "The remedies don't cure the disease, they prolong it."[5]

The only thing to do to really help—the true kindness—is to completely restructure society. Isn't that what Jesus came to do anyway? To flip tables in the temple and to reformulate an oppressive culture into one of freedom. Jesus did more than just hug away our differences. He completely changed faith and religion, ordering an end to the repressive hierarchies that saw widows, children, and the sick cast aside.

Love is political when it is radical. Faith is political when it believes in something better. Hope is political when it looks for something more.

In Bigelow, Minnesota, faith and politics collide, and history throbs against scars both literal and metaphorical. It's a place where history meets and the future is made. It isn't perfect, but Lord knows none of our efforts are. But Shirley's words still stay with me: "They are our friends." And I remember that the most powerful acts of Jesus were his gentle inclusions— when he spoke to a woman at the well, when he touched those who had been cast out. I don't believe that a hug can cure, but I do believe it is a start. And as much as I want Bigelow to be perfect, to be the exact answer, our faith call is not to be perfect, but to do our best. And that is what I see at Bigelow, a desire to be better, to do better.

9

BRIDGING THE DIVIDE

THERE WERE A DOZEN OF US IN THAT small beige room in Morton, Illinois. We were in a stone building, which sat just beyond the Walmart, where the town diffuses into farmland. The building is now the home of the Rural Home Missionary Association (RHMA), a nonprofit dedicated to training and equipping pastors to work and live in rural areas.

Ron Klassen stands at the front of the room, PowerPoint at the ready, and recites the statistics that inform RHMA's mission. Three out of four seminary graduates will pastor a church in a small town or country church. Most of the seminaries are in the cities. His lecture isn't news to us. It's June 25, 2017, and Donald Trump has been president for just over five months. We know America is divided, we can feel it, even in this room.

Out of the twelve of us, there are four women and eight men—and only one is a person of color. Two of the women are there in their role as pastor's wife. Another woman, Roberta, is in her mid-fifties and preparing for a second career as a pastor after a lengthy service in the military. I count as the fourth woman—I'm a journalist. During our class, Klassen and his teaching partner Barney Wells often comment how they've never had a group with so many women. The person of color is a male seminary student from Korea. And for the entirety of the course, we never talk about race.

The goal of the class is necessary but fraught. Wells and Klassen want to link the urban–rural divide using Evangelical pastors as the trestle. To that end, they have developed an entire curriculum to help the men in their classes understand rural America, including reading three different books on rural America and rural ministry, trips to a hog confinement and a dairy farm, a picnic with trapshooting, and a particularly unnerving exercise where we walk around a small town and try to talk to people.

This place and this curriculum are male-centric. RHMA is Evangelical and the majority of Evangelical churches in the Midwest do not ordain women. The bulk of the seminary students in the room come from Dallas Theological Seminary, an Evangelical seminary whose chancellor is Chuck Swindoll. Swindoll is a conservative heavy-hitter who is publicly against gay marriage, female pastors, and female elders. RHMA supports rural missionaries, and the application states that these missionaries must be men in heterosexual relationships. In order to attend the class, I had to sign a covenant stating that I wouldn't smoke or drink while I was there. I signed it, but I brought whiskey.

I knew what I was doing. My entire thirty-four years of life up to that point had been spent in the middle of America attending Evangelical churches. These spaces and beliefs were not foreign to me. I knew how to operate. I knew the coded language of words like "blessing" and "equipped" and "Biblical foundation." I had already attended NRA gun-safety training and was (and am, fight me) a crack shot. I'd been to hog confinements, and for many years my family bought our milk straight from a dairy farmer in Texas. I wasn't acting out of some sort of cultural ignorance. I knew exactly the world I was going into, and I knew, as well, that for the whole week, I was a woman alone in rural Illinois, with a group of conservative Christians, surrounded by cornfields and shoddy internet connection. That's exactly why I brought the whiskey and a sturdy pair of running shoes.

I was supposed to stay with a host couple, but at the last minute, at a gas station on the Iowa border, I decided to book a hotel room. I'm glad I did; it was a tough week. Bridging the rural–urban divide, as it turns out, requires emotional excavation.

* * *

On the first day of class, we begin with statistics. They were in our required reading, a textbook titled *Rural People and Communities in the Twenty-First Century*. It's clear pretty early on that I'm the only person who read the textbook. For those who hadn't, we go over the highlights with some PowerPoint slides for our aid.

The first problem is defining "rural," and this is a real problem. The US government defines rural as anything "not urban." It's a definition already in a negative, a delineation inside of an absence. An urban cluster area is any incorporated town with a population of more than "2,500 and less than 50,000 people."[1] Given that definition, only 15–30 percent of the population resides in a rural area.

But Klassen and Wells define "rural" a little differently. Their definition of rural includes any place with low population volume, low population density, extractive industry, and removal from goods and services. They show us a map of metro and nonmetro areas that show the parts of America removed from a large metropolitan area. With that definition, the territory of rural America increases.

The reality is more complicated. Rural is not just a census definition, it's a way of life. It's a mind-set that arises from the land. It's a way of thinking that is catalyzed by isolation and open spaces, by want, scarcity, nature, and family. By this definition, I am rural. But I don't say that out loud. No one would believe it from a journalist who has Jack Daniels in her bag and a keychain that reads "Feminist as Fuck."

The rural mind-set according, Klassen, is one that arises from land and place, but supersedes them. Therefore, he explains as he flips through slides, it makes sense that a pastor would preach while carrying a gun.

I visibly blanch. "Wait, explain that . . ."

Klassen smiles. Wells begins to tell a story about a pastor in rural Ohio who carried a gun at his hip every Sunday at the pulpit. Everyone in the room, except me, nods.

"Out here," Wells adds, "a gun isn't a weapon, it's a tool. You need it to hunt. You need it for your job. A gun is a pastoral aide."

Everyone is already on board with this logic. No other explanations are needed. It's almost as if Evangelicalism already has a predisposition to a rural buy-in. The language of this class is coded for political realities. For example, if I were to admit to everyone I voted for Clinton, I would immediately be cast as urban. And if this is the case, perhaps this class ought to be taught in reverse.

During a break I ask Klassen and Wells, "Can you teach this class in reverse? Can you teach rural people to understand urban life?" Klassen shakes his head and says he'll need to think about it. Wells frowns and explains that urbanism has been pushed on American culture for so long. What we need is ruralism. But he promises to think about the question and give me a better answer. I get that answer at the end of the week, when one of the pastors' wives calls me a sinner. But for now, we are strangers, sitting around a table, furiously trying to understand one another in a beige room that smells of stale Folgers and homemade shortbread.

The class is designed to be a mix of classroom and immersive experiences. So on our first night, we head out to the hobby farm of a local family,

John and Jane Sadler. Three generations of the Sadlers live on this sprawling acreage that has a pond, dug by the Sadler's son, Keith. The main house looks like a large toolshed, with an expansive awning over a slab of concrete. Wells tells us that John Sadler began his welding business in his machine shed. In order to skirt around property taxes and a whole bunch of other coding and zoning rules, he built up that shed as his house. He sold the business eleven years ago and has dedicated his retirement to serving the Lord. He donates his time and money to the church and opens his home to RHMA students every year. He also conducts life flights in his twin-engine airplane with Keith.

As we mill about eating plates of lasagna and salad, the Sadler's grandchildren, all in their late teens and early twenties, hover around, eager to help grab drinks, clean up the trash, and make sure their grandma is sitting down. In many ways, John Sadler is an archetypal Midwestern grandfather—a self-made jack-of-all-trades, he's vocal on politics and his theories on the apocalypse. I don't ask, but I know that if a TV is on inside the house, it's tuned to Fox News. There is a prayer before every meal. I know without being told that every single one of the people on this farm would give me clothes or money if I was in need.

Without going inside, I know the golden oak trim of the doorways, the worn La-Z-Boy chairs next to dated end tables that are overstuffed with pens, medicine, eye drops, and a half-finished crossword puzzle. I know these things because this is the home of every grandparent I've met in the twenty years I've lived in the Midwest—the comfortable, unpretentious hospitality, the pink carpet in the bathroom, and the cracked bars of soap that are probably older than you. I know it like I know cheesy potato casserole, and the way the goo of cheddar and cream of chicken soup radiates warmth from my stomach. It's a knowledge born of sensations rather than words, few of which are spoken. It's a memory of fading photographs on a yellowing fridge (no need to get a new fridge, they don't make them like they use to), homemade potato rolls, and powdered ice tea.

By any objective standards, the Sadlers are upper middle class, but they don't see it that way. They save, wash, and reuse tin foil.

I feel both at home and wildly out of place. I'm the journalist, not a pastor and not even married to one and at this point, not married for much longer. No one knows what to say to me. But I have kids, so I talk about them. The funny bon mots about my children are the safest conversational currency I have. I don't know what I'd do if I didn't have them to help set people at ease and bridge the divide that they already feel just by knowing that I'm a woman alone with an occupation. There is welcome, but there is also an unspoken reserve, and I spend a lot of time trying to put people at ease with my presence.

After we eat, Keith and his kids take us out trapshooting. I've been trapshooting since I was ten, but I keep this information to myself. It's early in the week, and already I need a win. I am the last in the lineup and spend my first turn warming up—miss three and hit two. Their expectations are low, so I get a lot of hearty congratulations. The second time I go up, I know the feel of the rifle and how it will kick into my shoulder. I know the glide of the action. I hit the first one. Reload. Yell, "Pull." Hit the second. Then the third. Then the fourth.

They see me now.

Keith is a big man—all muscle and white skin—who looks like he could be a cop on *The Shield*. "You say you are a pastor?" he asks as I eject the last cartridge, reload and take aim.

"No, just a writer," I say.

I hit the fifth clay pigeon. It's the end of the first day.

The next morning, we return to the topic of guns. William, a pastor in rural Illinois who has six kids, tells us, laughing, about the pastor he knows who preaches with a gun at his side. He must see me balk, because he turns to me and explains, "It's for safety, think about it, if someone were to run into the church with a gun, the pastor has the best line of fire."

I ask if this pastor is white and the room silences and William's eyes narrow in irritation. Of course he's white, "but it doesn't matter, does it?" he asks.

It does matter, but I say nothing. I still have four more days left. The conversation rights itself and they all tell stories of pastors with weapons. There is an unspoken danger in these tales, something lurking right outside of the walls of their faith. This danger goes by many names throughout the discussions—liberalism, atheism, bad moral character, immigrants, welfare, people who just don't understand. I'll meet this fear many times throughout the week, but even with all its names this fear never takes full shape. It's a faceless doom that feels tied to the land. Even though less than 2 percent of Americans are farmers, occupations here come from the land: mechanics who fix and build tractors, ag loan officers, feed store clerks. And the land is faithless—an ill-timed rain, a flood, a dry summer, or an early frost can spell disaster. All of those things make life here uneven. Doom. Apocalypse. Dread. It's all felt like a catch in the breath.

So there are guns. Wells takes over our conversation and now it's time to learn. We all take out our pens and write down his words. He says, "Guns are a way of life born of necessity from a time when guns were necessary for protecting livestock and oneself from predators. It would take the police over 15 minutes to get to some of these farms. Guns are for protection. Now, they are like basketball, a recreational sport." Wells continues. "In the city, guns are used in crimes. That's why cosmopolitan people object to them. But here guns are just a normal way of life. If you are going to minister to a rural congregation, you have to get over your gun hang ups."

There is a couple in this group. They are from Canada and, like me, they stink of liberalism. They are vegetarians and interested in sustainable farming practices. Wells and Klassen have already told them that they might need to get over their vegetarianism because being a vegetarian in a place where people's occupation is focused on livestock could be offensive. Give it up. Go underground. Maybe just practice that lifestyle in your own home. Don't push it on other people. Right now, like me, they shift in their seats uncomfortably during the gun conversation. But we say nothing. The message has always been clear: To bridge this divide, you must die to yourself. Become other than yourself. But how much of a person's difference is a choice they can hide, and how much of it is who they are, and what is the cost of hiding? We don't talk about it.

That night I go for a four-mile run along the road that goes straight by the Walmart and into the soybean fields and back. This is a place build around the land, but there are no jogging paths. All pedestrian sidewalks end in the empty lots behind car dealerships or run into the parking lot of fast food restaurants and never come out again. I run on the side of the road and the whole time, I feel like I am going to die. I don't belong on this side of the road. I am not from this town. People driving by must wonder who I am, whose daughter is visiting? Whose cousin from out of town? Trucks driven by boys with square jaws run by me a little too close. When I get back to the hotel, I have some whiskey and go straight to bed.

Much of what we talk about in class is religious history told slant. Barney Wells divides American history into two halves: Jeffersonian and Hamiltonian. Jeffersonian ideals value land and the communities around them, while a Hamiltonian perspective, Wells tells us, favors cities and a strong central government. Wells mocks this Hamiltonian ideal, "Everyone thinks we should live in big cities and the government should tell us what to do." The tone of his voice makes it clear that he thinks that is wrong.

There are threads of logic not being pulled here. Ones about race and inclusion. How Jefferson didn't see slaves as humans. How landowners meant the white people and the wealthy. How this Hamiltonian ideal was designed to take power out of the hands of a landed gentry, to be divided more equally among the people.

Everyone in the class is writing furiously, drinking it all in. I look up to see if my friends the vegetarians have raised their hands, but nothing. Die to self. I'm here to understand. So I write it all down.

Wells and Klassen have developed a taxonomy of understanding rural landscapes and what the shape of a church will tell you about the people in town. A soaring gothic steeple in the center of town means it's Catholic, which means, as Wells notes as an aside, there is a more liberal attitude toward drinking, the reverence of objects, and family is the center of life. "Faith is . . ." he says and shrugs. We are all meant to guess what that means. Growing up Evangelical, I interpret his vagueness to mean that he thinks faith and morality are performative in a Catholic town.

If it's a small white traditional church on the edge of the town, it's Lutheran. The town is clean and well cared for. Family is also important. Hard work is a value. Aesthetics are important.

An apostolic church is theologically conservative, aesthetics are not important, but repentance is. It's assumed, Klassen says tagging in, that the young people will "experience the world." Then they will grow up and have kids and turn good again.

Faith for Wells and Klassen are essential to their understanding of place. And they aren't wrong in a way; in every place we visit during the week of class, schools don't have activities on Wednesday nights out of deference to church activities and on Sundays almost everything is closed. This is true in my town too, Cedar Rapids. Faith affiliation and church defines social circles and activities. Church is for Girl Scout gatherings, first aid classes, baby showers, and wedding showers. When a church is gone or closed, there is a void left in the collective identity of the town.

A taxonomy of churches is the key to understanding the people here. Even in ways that are indirect. Klassen and Wells pepper their lectures with stories about their own experiences as pastors of rural congregations in the Midwest. Even those who don't go to church on a regular basis, Klassen and Wells tell us, in the Midwest still feel faith woven into their lives. This is most evident, on the fourth day, when we visit a soybean farm-er, who tells us how his field feels like his church, it's how he encounters creation and the Lord. He's shy when he says this, a sixty-year-old man, who scuffs the ground with his boots, while he says the most beautiful words of the week.

But for now, on the third day, Klassen and Wells talk about men who never step foot in the church but come to plow the pastor's driveway during a blizzard.

After this lecture, it's time to put this taxonomy to work. We are div-ided into groups, given towns to research, and bused out to communities. It's an awkward cultural exercise in understanding your own country. For the entire rest of the day, I want to crawl inside myself and disappear.

The town we stop in is so small that Wells walks into the police station to let them know we are coming. He doesn't want residents seeing swarms of people (all twelve of us) downtown and calling the police—this has hap-pened before to another group. These places are small, everyone knows everyone. A new car would attract enough attention for a local cop to keep an eye on it. We are in a giant bus. We pile out, we are supposed to talk to people—buy something, have an interaction. Couples and the men who are there without their spouses partner up. No one seems to want to be near me, so I walk to the grocery store to buy a bag of chips.

It's just afternoon on a Tuesday in June. With the exception of a bar and the grocery store, no shops are open. I see someone open their curtains and look out at us from an apartment above a store front. I wave. The curtains shut. The store beneath is a kind of junk store—the windows are filled with plastic dolls, a wooden chair draped with beads and a large Confederate flag hanging in the background. Illinois, billed "the Land of Lincoln," was firmly in the Union during the Civil War. That flag is not there for even superficial history reasons. It's there as a symbol.

I feel people watching me as I go to the grocery store, but I don't ever see anyone else besides my classmates. I feel afraid to walk into a place, any place, alone. I'm a woman. I'm a journalist. I don't have the cloak of moral-ity of a pastor. I've already felt hostility from my own classmates. I wonder if this is why the group is so white. If I didn't have the mantle of my skin color, how much more would I be afraid? The Confederate flag is a clue. The way the male clerk in the store eyes me and how my skin turns clammy in response is another clue. The drawn curtain is another. The town is a clenched fist.

I buy my chips and a soda and go back to the bus. Eating on a bench in front of a bar, I hear two of my classmates emerge from behind the heavy black door, chatting loudly with the people inside. They made a connection—of course they did—because they are white middle-aged men. They wear the right clothes, they can announce they are pastors—the currency of their morality, cashed in like so many large bills.

On the bus again, William tells us how great it was. How friendly people were. How willing to talk. I begin to wonder if this is my fault. I didn't even try. But the idea of walking into a bar as a woman alone in that town makes my stomach churn. I'd done it before a few weeks prior, on my way back from a trip to Thurman, Iowa. It was my own kind of cultural experiment—walk in, order something unobtrusive, see if someone will talk to me about faith.

I'd done it. I walked in, I got lots of stares, but no one said anything except the bartender, a woman in her fifties who gave me a Miller Lite and suggested I leave. "You might want to head out before the next crowd comes in, honey," she said. She was being kind. It was the sort of offering women give each other about safety and social cues. I finished my beer and left. The three men at the bar didn't ever stop watching the television, until my back was to them. I could see the reflection of their eyes in the door refracting a warning.

In her book *Those Who Work, Those Who Don't: Poverty, Morality, and Family in Rural America*, Jennifer Sherman posits that in places lacking resources, morality is social capital. Appearing "good" unlocks jobs and community resources. But morality is determined in a fluid way; it's just as much about fitting in and looking the part as it is about good behavior. Being white, wearing the right clothes (not too fancy, not too dirty), being male, being married, and having children were all part of the appearance of morality. But it wasn't just about "good" behavior. John Sadler had stretched the law in an extra-legal way to get around the tax code. But this was looked on as an example of good behavior—he was conning the government after all. This made him smart and quick-witted, a cunning businessman and someone you would respect. Hell, he was a leader in his community.

While I was a white woman, I wasn't occupying the right spaces, with my dyed hair, my ironic t-shirts, ripped jeans, I may have still had a ring on my finger at that point and pictures of children to show to recalcitrant strangers, but my moral capital was occupying a dissonant space merely because I was a woman alone. A woman out on a job. A journalist. Ron and Barney were building a bridge, but the only people who were allowed on it were white, cisgendered men.

That night I go for another run. Again the trucks run too close and I feel my body occupying a space between the mortality of the road and the emptiness of the fields. When I come back to the room, I turn on the TV. The news stories all tell me about our divided nation. I change the channel. I already know our nation is divided, the divide exists in me. In the way I both fit and don't fit. The ways I am both moral and abhorrent.

I feel the divide in my marriage, my husband's growing reluctance to even talk to me about my writing or my work. A month after the trip, he will send me an email asking me to quit everything. Quit this project. Quit writing. The only parts of me he wants to see are me as a mother and as a wife.

I feel the divide in my body—in the way the muscles in my neck throb from smiling a smile I don't believe in at that mom from school. The divide aches in me the way my head throbs when a thunderstorm builds. I turn the channel to one of the many crime shows that populate TV. It could have been *Forensic Files*, I don't know. I don't remember, because I'm not paying attention. I take a shower and swallow a shot of whiskey, no more than one shot. It's not about the drink really, it's about uniting my disparate parts, it's about the hot burn down my throat. I'm not building a bridge, I'm burning a wall. It's a hot rebellion, sliding down my center. Each swallow is a violation of the contract I signed—it's a break, a destruction of a barrier, and it makes me feel whole.

Earlier in the day, Barney Wells had told us all that we needed to give up to blend in with rural America. We must die to our sinful selves, was the message. We must assimilate to the culture. After he is finished, the class is filled with hypotheticals about food, clothing, jewelry, and dairy restrictions. Everyone is suddenly worried that they cannot be themselves in their own country.

Klassen fielded these questions with a parable. He recalled a time as a pastor in rural Nebraska when his family was invited over for lunch at the home of a member of the congregation. The kids ate first and when they were done, the parents picked up a dirty plate and filled it with food. Those dirty plates, Ron realized, were for him and his wife, because there weren't enough clean ones for everyone. With only a slight hesitation, Ron and his wife picked up the plates of their children, filled them with food, and ate.

The room was silenced.

The message was clear: To connect, you must cede body and soul to where you are. You cannot resist. And what about the markers we cannot hide or we cannot change without losing ourselves—skin color or gender? For some, clothes are utilitarian, an easy switch to make, for others clothes are an armor, a protection against the eyes and hands that have damaged them so many times before. For me, my hair is a flag—I began dying it after my second child was born, spending too much money to make it red, then blue, then blonde, and black with purple highlights. There is a force to it, an anger. It's a response to a request for homogeneity in my own personal life—to cede to the values of my husband, to go to the church he wants, to stay silent when the pastor condemns gay marriage from the pulpit, to avoid writing about difference in my work. In this moment, as I sit in the classroom, I am trying to acquiesce. Dave and I have been in counseling on and off for two years. Trying to build a bridge, but my body is the only one bending. That of course is a metaphor, but there is literal truth to it. I've lost over twenty pounds. I've been running so hard, I'm sometimes afraid I'll break and sometimes I don't think that's a bad thing. A month and a half after this class, I will break emotionally and ask for a divorce. But in that room, I am trying. And in that room I am failing.

I know the costs of hiding. I've had to hide for so much of my life—hide my doubt, hide my opinions. I don't do it well—ask anyone. In the room, I'm trying to hide how I feel, so I keep eating shortbread cookies, filling my mouth, just so I can listen. But my jaw aches. I feel the divide again in my body. I know what it is like to live in a place where visible difference is ground down through rejection and isolation. Homogeneity is a comfort only for those for whom it is built. For the rest of us, it is destabilizing, not unlike trying to hide a beach ball under the water with your entire body. No matter how hard you work, the air in the ball rises, the force of the water pushes you off and off. To hide the ball would mean destroying it. How good is a place, how big are its horizons, if there isn't room for everyone? There isn't room for everyone in this class.

On our penultimate day together, the men have a break, while the women are sent off to have lunch with Ron's wife, Nancy. The goal of the talk is to discuss how pastors' wives support their husbands in a rural environment. Except half of us are not pastors' wives, and Roberta, who is a pastor herself, chafes against the box she's being put in.

"I don't know why I'm here," she says as we all fill our plates from a homemade salad bar. No one answers her. She continues. "I'm a pastor."

Someone coughs.

I offer up a platitude. "They must not have many female pastors, they don't seem to know what to do with you."

There is another pause. "Let's pray for this lunch," Nancy says.

It's a suggestion that builds a wall. No one wants this conversation. We pray. We drink iced tea and choose the healthiest toppings for our salads. We've had a week of meat and potatoes. We talk about children. A wife of one of the other pastors is there, joining us just for the lunch, she tells us how she has to be careful what she posts on Facebook because the community is so small and people criticize her husband if she posts positively about something like Harry Potter. I stab at sunflower seeds. I smile.

Later that evening, I give Roberta a ride back to the house where she is staying, and in the car she explains that she's exhausted from the whole week. "I'm used to this, I was in the military," she explains. But it was different in the military; if she was good she could advance, and she did. Here her goodness, her moral capital, has taken a hit because she's a woman assuming a role traditionally filled by a man. She explains to me how angry she felt when we did a role-playing game. How all the men played the roles of church leaders—pastors, deacons, elders—how all the women were ascribed roles as Sunday school teachers, wives, secretaries.

"If this is the Midwest, if this is America, maybe I don't want to be a pastor here," she tells me. I cannot disagree with her. Not really.

I know a lot of female pastors who live and work in Middle America, who occupy these spaces of moral dissonance. But I know it isn't easy work and it's filled with the constant questioning and bending and breaking. She knows that too, better than me. I look at her and wonder at all that her body endured to exist in a place that is so masculine. Where she had to prove herself through physicality. She is bigger and stronger. We have hardly talked all week. But we've been thrust together—discussion groups, car rides, and we would have been roommates had I not booked a hotel. We have nothing in common besides being oddball white ladies.

I know that there is a hope within both of us that it should be better by now. That the realities of who we are should not be a barrier to the places we want to occupy. But they are. And that's the one bridge we cannot build, the one that erases our humanity.

I put the car in park and offer her the only thing I can, an apology. "I'm sorry," I say. "You are right to be angry."

Roberta has come here to be a bridge, to learn how to unite a divided America. She's a white woman, she has a military career, but it's not enough. Who she is isn't enough. We sit in silence for just a moment before Roberta opens the door and asks me to give her a false name if I write about this. She doesn't want to be part of this story. She's been part of stories like this too many times.

* * *

On the last day, I ask my question again, this time to everyone in the group, "Can this class be taught in reverse?"

I want to know if a class can be taught for rural people to build a bridge to city people. I imagine it looking like trips to fancy department stores, talking to Wall Street bankers and journalists. Some of my classmates nod vigorously. Others shift uncomfortably in their chairs. Ron tells another parable. There was a class like this taught by a seminary in a rural Southern state. They would bus students into New York City, talk to people who lived in high-rises, interview a sales associate at Calvin Klein. "Did the class also emphasize the goodness of city values?" I ask. I'm kind of kidding but mostly not. This is when one of the wives snaps. I think she's had it with me from a long week. Her eyes flare up. "City values are sinful!" she yells.

I'm not surprised. I feel like this has been the subtext this whole week. A subtle push in the direction of rural, which has been defined by all the good buzzwords of American society—wholesome, connected to the land, family values, independent, and self-made.

But Ron poses a question. "Is it a sin to buy a $100,000 tractor if you need it for your job? What then about a $100,000 suit?"

No one answers. The class is over and we all go home.

10

A DEN OF THIEVES

And Jesus went into the temple of God, and cast out all them that
sold and bought in the temple, and overthrew the tables of the
moneychangers, and the seats of them that sold doves, And said
unto them, "It is written, My house shall be called the house of
prayer; but ye have made it a den of thieves."

Matthew 21:12–13

THE SPIRE OF WOODDALE CHURCH RISES LIKE A wiry alien over the 212
highway in Eden Prairie, Minnesota. In high school, when I attended
youth group at Wooddale, I told everyone it was a giant middle finger to
God. I was just being an asshole seventeen-year-old conflicted about religion and this new world I had been thrust into, but now at thirty-five, I still
feel the same.

My family moved from Vermillion, South Dakota, to Eden Prairie,
Minnesota, in the middle of my junior year of high school. In a matter of
weeks, I went from going to a school with five hundred students to one with
three thousand. The parking lot of the high school had Volvos and Mer-
cedes. The fanciness of the cars were downplayed with "My dad just wants
me to have a safe car." The teacher's lot was filled with busted up Hondas
and Toyotas. I rode the bus.

The median income in Eden Prairie is $105,868, nearly $40,000 above
the median for the state. In Vermillion, the median income is $32,584, near-
ly $20,000 below the state average. In Vermillion, I could walk anywhere or
hitch rides with my friends in their clunky, hand-me-down Fords. But in
Eden Prairie, the only things walkable were the nature trails, which didn't
take you anywhere useful. Their function was to get you away from the gray

swoops of highway and busy traffic of the city. (It's such a rich-person as-
sumption to believe that sidewalks should take you away from, rather than
to, somewhere.) I did get rides sometimes, but my friends grew tired of my
neediness.

"Just ask your parents for a car," they'd tell me. They understood the
stock market better than they understood the economics of poverty and of
living in a house with seven brothers and sisters. So I learned to quit asking
and just stopped showing up to things.

If high school culture was almost inaccessible without wealth, then
church was even more so. There weren't buses to church. My parents began
attending Wooddale, the nondenominational megachurch in 2000. Leith
Anderson was the pastor and had been since 1977. Under his leadership,
Wooddale had grown from a moderately sized church with a weekly attendance of around 250 in 1959 to a church with an average weekly attendance
of 5,500. They'd built a new building and expanded their worship offerings.

By the time my family and I began attending, the church was so large it
felt like a stadium. Worship featured impeccably dressed men and women
warbling at impossible ranges. Lights. Video. Even the high school room
had a set up more professional than the local community theater.

Food was regularly collected for the homeless, but the homeless rarely
found their way through our doors. How could they? Without a car, the
church was nearly impenetrable. And if you managed to get inside, the sea
of smooth white skin and glistening hair and broad straight smiles were
enough to make anyone who didn't fit in feel intimidated.

I didn't fit in. I moved to Minnesota with an arsenal of thrift-store flannel shirts and ripped jeans with Marxist slogans I had scrawled on them in
black sharpie. My parents did their best, buying me Gap jeans and T-shirts
from J. Crew. And it worked, but the cost of belonging was assimilation in a
place that should have been big enough for all.

Big churches are big business in the Midwest. Many studies show that
of the approximately 384,000 churches in America,[1] between 5 percent and
10 percent average more than one thousand members.[2] Ed Stetzer, pastor
and church planter, estimates that the number of megachurches has nearly
doubled every ten years in the last century.[3] While most of America's largest
megachurches are in the South, three of the top ten states for megachurches
are in the Midwest: Illinois, Indiana, and Ohio. Megachurches might not
be a way of life here, but they are growing and they are changing how Midwesterners conceive of their faith and their role in culture.

For people longing for community and connection, megachurches make sense. They are like small cities—they offer summer camps, sports programs, daycare, and even schools. Some have restaurants and coffee shops. They offer intentional communities built around moral sameness, which gives families safe harbor in a lonely, modern, and dangerous world. Built-in friendships and safety come at just the cost of your tithe. There are enough people there to offer the programing you want, but the small groups and Bible studies scale it down to the size you need. But megachurches come at a cost.

The biggest impact is that these big churches draw from smaller ones—the Walmart effect. Big-box religion is shutting down smaller churches and the feud is palpable. During my interviews, many pastors cited large churches in cities as a huge draw for their local communities. The criticism goes the other way too. In 2016, Andy Stanly, pastor of North Point Community Church in Georgia, raged against small churches, noting:

> When I hear adults say, "Well, I don't like a big church. I like about 200, I want to be able to know everybody," I say, "You are so stinkin' selfish. You care nothing about the next generation. All you care about is you and your five friends. You don't care about your kids, anybody else's kids." . . . I'm saying if you don't go to a church large enough where you can have enough Middle Schoolers and High Schoolers to separate them so they can have small groups and grow up the local church, you are a selfish adult. Get over it. Find yourself a big old church where your kids can connect with a bunch of people and grow up and love the local church.[4]

Stanly later apologized for his remarks, but the battle lines still remain drawn.

Bigger churches are a draw precisely because of their size; they offer more programming, more opportunities for Bible studies, community groups, and intramural sports. In many ways, they resemble the small communities they are decimating, except these are communities created around identity rather than geography. Christianity has always been tribal—creating identity and community out of orthodoxy. But megachurches have a way of distilling that tribal identity and weaponizing it.

* * *

There is a lot of marketing copy and sermonizing put into declaring megachurches a new invention. Lyle Schaller, a church consultant, wrote in *Christianity Today*, "The emergence of the 'megachurch' is the most important development of modern Christian history. You can be sentimental about the small congregation, like the small corner grocery store or small drugstore, but they simply can't meet the expectations that people carry with them today."[5]

But as David Eagle argues in his 2015 paper "Historicizing the Megachurch," that large institutional worship has a long history beginning in the Protestant Reformation. He describes how in 1601, Huguenot architect Jacques Perret outlined a large-scale church where "three levels of ancillary spaces to accommodate secular and religious purposes surrounded the temple."[6] This grand vision was never built, but the design inspired other churches and, more importantly, began locating the process of making the church more about commerce and less about God. Eagle writes, "Written around the outside of Perret's temple we find the slogan, 'The Christian children of God are his true temple.' The building is still grand and ornate, but it is no longer the locus of God's activity. This opens up the possibility that the church building can now play an important role in the wider political and cultural sphere."[7]

In the mid-nineteenth century, Charles Spurgeon's Metropolitan Tabernacle in London was built to hold six thousand. Other revivalist churches were built to be large and expansive. The Baptist Temple in Philadelphia was built in 1891, and as Eagle describes it, was almost a community into and of itself.

> The Temple boasted a college; one of the best-equipped gymnasiums in Philadelphia; a nearby cricket field and baseball diamond; an affiliated Hospital (to which the Sunday services were broadcast over special speaking tubes); a separate 'Young People's Church,' which met in the basement and could accommodate 2,000; a large banquet facility; and regular concerts, lectures, debates, and readings in its main sanctuary. As Loveland and Wheeler note, "The church's founder, Russel H. Cornwell, justified the Temple's sponsorship of 'entertainments' on the grounds that the church should use 'any reasonable means to influence men for good.'"[8]

There were others too, even before the mix of capitalism, industrialism, and corporate culture permeated America, making us believe in the power of bigger is better. The gospel of size isn't particularly new. The New Testament book of Acts tells the story of Pentecost, when the Holy Spirit comes down to the new disciples and gives them the ability to speak and teach in different languages. The chapter ends with this promise: "Every day they continued to meet together in the temple courts. They broke bread in their homes and ate together with glad and sincere hearts, praising God and enjoying the favor of all the people. And the Lord added to their number daily those who were being saved."

Growth in church numbers indicates favor from the Lord.

Never was this gospel more true than in post–World War II America, booming with jobs and cheap goods. Megachurches began to pop up around celebrity preachers—Billy Graham did the most to become a center of corporate Christianity. Linking together the Christian ethic with the American ethos. In 1955, he preached to an American Legion post, "Recognition of a Supreme Being is the first and most basic expression of Americanism." And because Graham learned early on that speaking on current events would draw a bigger crowd, his sermons were rife with political commentary. He filled stadiums wherever he preached, wrote a weekly newspaper column, and had a weekly radio message. The Billy Graham Evangelistic Association estimates that throughout his lifetime, Graham preached the gospel to more than 215 million people in more than 185 countries and territories—even more when including video and film recordings. During these sermons, Graham was relentlessly political. He called Truman "cowardly."[9] In 1952, he told a crowd that the Korean War had been fought because Alger Hiss had never been East; and he complimented the McCarthy committee, noting, "I thank God for the men and women who, in the face of public denouncement and ridicule, go loyally on in their work of exposing the pinks, the lavenders and the reds who have sought refuges beneath the wings of the American eagle."[10]

In his book *One Nation Under God*, Kevin Kruse, professor of history at Princeton University, weaves a damning portrait of the way Evangelical populism intertwined itself with conservative capitalism and politics. He describes how, in response to the anticorporate sentiment of the New Deal, American industrialists found a champion in the libertarian spirituality of conservative Christianity. Spurred on by the reactions to communism, which was equated with liberal socialism, Christianity, Americanism, and capitalism became the Father, Son, and Holy Ghost of America.

Many early pastors and spiritual leaders played a role in blending these elements, but none so effectively as Billy Graham. A beloved spiritual scion, Graham courted power in all realms—Christian, corporate, and political. A proto-megachurch pastor, Graham drew the large crowds that gave evidence of success. Much like amassing a fortune showed signs of God's favor, Graham amassed crowds, and canny politicians and businessmen saw the potent potential of his purifying appeal.

Graham was an evangelist and not a megachurch pastor, but he provided the prototype. In his wake, other personalities like Jerry Falwell, Charles Dobson, James Kennedy, Bill Hybels, Rick Warren, Robert Jeffress, Eric Metaxas, Tony Perkins, Ralph Reed, and Graham's own son Franklin took up the model—corporate Christianity, married to conservativism, channeled through large powerful churches.

While only 10 percent of worshippers attend a megachurch, the cultural influence of the megachurch pastors knows no bounds. Not only do they have their congregations, but these pastors also have blogs, videos, books, podcasts, social media, and more, which provide a wide-reaching platform for their largely white, heterosexual, corporately conservative Christianity to thrive. Their message is validated by their popularity—popular because they are successful, successful because they are popular.[11]

Yet, walk into almost any of these churches and you'll hear sermons about how Christians are an oppressed minority. It would be laughable—white, upper-middle-class Christians proclaiming their oppression—if it weren't in earnest. Having popularity and influence, but somehow still insisting on its existence on the margins. It's an amazing magic trick, and one enabled by people like me, Christians horrified by the connection between Evangelicalism and conservative politics. We want to believe that this isn't us, so we yell, "THIS ISN'T US!" There is no end to the books and articles declaring the death of this pernicious Evangelical culture. Surely if we call it dead enough times, it will die.

But this only fuels its popularity. In their book *The Churching of America*, Roger Finke and Rodney Stark argue that specific spiritual movements in America thrive because of their conservative appeal and they decline once they "liberalize." In essence, in a world of uncertainty, conservative spirituality offers a strong prescription for what it means to live a life of faith and be good. The constant conflict, as well as competition, fuels their sense of righteousness. The more we declare their death, the faster they grow.

Finke and Stark point out that after the Scopes Monkey Trial, Americans were quick to declare the death of what they labeled an anti-intellectual strain of fundamentalism. But instead of dying, it just created its own subculture, one that is strong and powerful and thrives on the perception of marginalization.

While writing this book, I wrote to Roger Finke to ask him if he'd amend his findings in the wake of the 2016 election. Surely, I wanted to know, this wasn't good. Right? Surely, it would end. I wanted Finke to tell me it was over. That whatever Evangelicalism in America had become it would now end, once it held office. But Finke, ever the academic, refused to moralize, instead noting broadly, "During times of conflict the 'radical' groups can find motivation and generate allegiance from religious teachings." He put radical in quotations. The perception of radicalism. The perception of counter-culturalism. That's all it needs. The common enemy of the percieved mainstream.

Once, at a birthday party, a fellow school mom confided to me that she felt America, especially the Midwest, was on the decline. She'd just come back from a trip to Charleston, South Carolina, where she'd seen people "boldly proclaiming their faith with Jesus T-shirts" and even business signs, she said, had the Lord's name on them. This white upper-middle-class woman, who sent her kids to private school, proceeded to explain how Christians in the Midwest were oppressed because we didn't have the boldness to wear these shirts and put these signs up in our own towns. She was on the margins and nothing I said could shake that core belief. In fact, I'm sure I only solidified it.

And this is despite the fact that white Evangelicals, fueled by mega-church pastors, are largely responsible for Donald Trump's presidency. The cover story for the April 2018 issue of *The Atlantic* was titled "The Last Temptation," with the subtitle, "How evangelicals, once culturally confident, became an anxious minority seeking political protection from the least traditionally religious president in living memory."

So much winning, all while declaring themselves losers.

The cycle continues.

* * *

Megachurches sell a dangerous lie—one gobbled up too easily by white middle-class Americans. Parading as independent, these churches are actually conservative cultural centers. They sell an easy brand of corporate Christianity—stylish moms and clean-shaven men in flannel who play guitars. The pastors talk about Snapchat, the worship has cool lights and really great vocals. The decor looks like a Hobby Lobby vomited all over the place—replica barnwood, faux vintage hooks, exposed beams, a chalkboard that tells you "God is good," and coffee is $.25.

Everyone here loves Chip and Joanna Gaines. Men have scruffy beards. The women have great highlights. All the kids wear organic cotton. It would be easy to believe you could fit in here. There are Sunday schools for all the kids, community groups, and even a discussion group that meets in a bar. A bar! But scratch the surface and the ideology is conservative Christianity made marketable for the white upper middle class.

Attending a church like this in Cedar Rapids was a comfortable compromise for Dave and I after our church closed. It was an easy place to heal, I thought, from the wounds of the orthodoxies that had been leveled at me at our previous church. And for a while it was, in that I was virtually ignored. When sermons were given that condemned abortion or sarcastically chided liberals for PC speech, I just got up and left. After all, even though we didn't agree on perspective or politics, we were all on this faith journey together.

God was God, I reminded myself. We are all his children.

But when a pastor preached a sermon condemning divorce in all circumstances, I sent him an email. A good friend of mine was going through a divorce because of years of horrific abuse; what about that instance, I asked? What about Grace? And also, I noted, women who heard messages like this preached from the pulpit might not go to their pastors for help if they needed it.

I heard nothing in response.

A few months later, there was the shooting at the Pulse nightclub in Orlando. I brought my family to church that Sunday, my heart torn apart for my friends, for America.

My pastor said nothing.

During 2016, the pastors of this church mentioned the nineteen-year-old man who tried to pull a gun on Donald Trump at a campaign rally, they led us in prayers for slain police officers, and they gave sermons lamenting growing Islamic fundamentalism, they told jokes about Hillary Clinton's emails, made prayerful references to the acceptance of gay marriage as evidence of America's eroding moral core, but gave no mention of Philando Castile and the numerous men and women shot by the police. Nothing about Donald Trump's pussy-grabbing comments. (But, of course, a joke or two had been made about the Clintons' morals during the year.)

Christianity in America is under attack, was the message given only a few weeks before the election. The implications were clear to anyone who was listening—conservatism was the dog whistle rising others to the call. Women and men who found Donald Trump otherwise deplorable voted for him out of their conscience, because of abortion, because of gay marriage, because of the "attacks" on Christianity. It wasn't hard to make the connections.

The next year, during the attack on Charlottesville my church again was silent and I'd had enough.

Every Sunday I'd walk in with my two children, a boy and a girl, my husband, and shake the hands of other similarly perfect couples—we'd talk about microbrews, the new hamburger place that opened in town, someone's Etsy store, someone else's cover band, never acknowledging that my soul was screaming one big giant "WHAT THE FUCK IS GOING ON?!"

While the world outside cried and bled, while we felt the turmoil of a historic election thrust on us, nothing changed inside the church—their message was that "God was unchangeable," an otherwise sound maxim, but the theology was nothing more than a justification for white privilege.

It was a twisted theology. "I don't want to be political" people would demur when I eventually blurted out something like a human Mt. Vesuvius—splattering the lava of my opinions all over this sacred space. It's a disingenuous disavowal. Ever since the New Deal, Christianity and politics have made the pulpit a complicated place. Preachers and faith leaders like Billy Graham and Jerry Falwell have long made political commentary the business of the pulpit. But as with the sermons, it's about what goes unsaid. Because while the people in this church demurred about politics, from the pulpit came an onslaught of opinions about the evils of abortion and gay marriage. While federal law prohibits clergy from endorsing political candidates, many still speak out on social issues such as poverty, abortion, religious liberty, and homosexuality. A study by the Pew Center on Religion and Public Life found that of church-going Americans, two-thirds had heard politics preached from the pulpit. And with the majority of white Evangelicals voting for Donald Trump in 2016, it's not hard to parse what the politics are that they are hearing.

One night, at dinner with friends we'd met at this church, I raised the issue of politics. I told them I was bothered by the omissions—the conservative dog whistle that was making my ears bleed.

The couple looked at one another in confusion.

"We hadn't even noticed," the wife said.

I wondered what would have happened if the tables were reversed. What if the politics being preached were liberal? But I knew the answer.

After that, I asked my then husband if we could leave. We tried another church and it was just more of the same, but in a smaller church with shittier carpet and instead of a beer ministry there was an AA group that met every Wednesday. My kids hated it. I hated it. Nothing was that different.

So, we went back to the big church and I sent an email to the pastors asking to meet. We should discuss their politics and doctrine at least, I felt. I wanted to hear their position on the matter, to ask questions, to interrogate what I was being asked to swallow. No one replied. The silences were louder than screams.

Church is supposed to be a place of community, where together we try to figure out how to live and love and grapple with the great mystery of what it means to be human. It should be a place that provides harbor from storms, not a place that uses white privilege to pretend those storms don't exist.

After the Charlottesville attack, I left the church and began attending a small ELCA church in my neighborhood, where one pastor was gay, the other was a woman, and they both listened to my concerns. The church held a prayer service after the Charlottesville attack, and I saw the head pastor at a rally that Sunday, when I stood up on a cement retaining wall at a park in the middle of town and shouted that as people of faith we ought to be angry about what was being done in our name.

"We are Midwesterners, we don't like to be angry. But Jesus flipped tables when he saw the temple turned into a den of thieves, the least we can do is raise our voices." Yet, even while I shouted into a crowd, while faith leaders from different area churches applauded me, I was afraid of my husband learning about what I was doing. I knew I had to leave. But I also knew the cost.

When I left that church, I left alone. When I left that church, what I left was my marriage. I guess I could have stayed—at my church and in my marriage—if I was willing to be silent. If I was willing to sit in the pew, hold my thoughts close to my chest, and never even gently nudge over a table. I'm ashamed that Charlottesville was my tipping point. White privilege is a hell of a drug.

* * *

Megachurches represent the epitome of white Evangelical privilege—centers by and through which fantastical narratives are created and entire histories and people are erased. During my senior year of high school, the youth pastor at Wooddale disappeared. His name was CJ and I remember him as someone who saw me. In an entire church where I felt lost and had been asked several times by staff and volunteers to "talk less" in group situations, CJ listened. In hindsight, this wasn't radical, it was his job. But the entire youth group had just as many kids as had attended my high school in South Dakota. And I was a teen who wrote Marxist slogans on her jeans and had to take the bus while everyone else drove cars. Just the fact that he, a pastor, was listening—it felt like everything. I told him I wanted to be a pastor and even though the church did not affirm women as head pastors, he told me to follow my call.

One Sunday, I came to youth group and he was gone, in his place was a bizarro version of CJ. CJ was slight and blond with a crew cut, his replacement was slight and blond, but with long shaggy hair. CJ had been soft spoken and wore preppy clothes—khakis, jeans, and polos—while his replacement was loud and wore stained T-shirts and ripped jeans. It was like a television show replacing a beloved character without first offering a narrative for their disappearance. Well, were we expected not to notice? We did notice, but no one told us anything. Staff and volunteers told us to talk to our parents, and our parents, for the most part, were tight lipped.

There were a lot of rumors, which all centered around an inappropriate relationship with an eighteen-year-old girl in the youth group. But whatever had happened, whatever the truth was, it was disappeared along with the girl, it was treated with silence. Like it had never happened. A few years ago, I asked someone who worked at Wooddale about CJ. The situation had been handled, she assured me. He had been disciplined by the church elders. But what about the girl, I wanted to know? What about the rest of us?

"Why talk about it?" she asked.

This is why. Because while CJ was being swept under the rug, one of my sisters was being sexually abused by someone close to her. We wouldn't know for five more years about what was happening. She wouldn't feel safe telling us. She didn't need to be taught her silence, it was all around her.

This is how power works.

It twists and pulls the ranges of who we are and who we are supposed to be—limiting us not just by its restrictions but through its silences and subtleties.

The Evangelical #ChurchToo movement, is a movement dedicated to fighting the Christian power structures that enable abuse in the church. Started by Hannah Paasch and Emily Joy, the movement began on Twitter and has called to account the actions of prominent church leaders like Bill Hybels, Memphis Megachurch pastor Andy Savage, Chris Conlee of Highpoint Church, and others. But Becca Andrews, writing in *Mother Jones*, argues that the problem is still pervasive. "As I've written before, strict gender roles, the value that is placed on sexual purity for women in particular, and the godly celebrity afforded to many of these often white, often male megachurch preachers all contribute to the problem that reaches well beyond Highpoint and Willow Creek."[12]

The problem of the megachurch is the problem of the faceless corporation—the problem of power. The way it twists a narrative, the way it controls a region, the way it flattens and assimilates, expects adherence and capitulation. Challenges are ignored. And the story that is told is a tight flat circle—those who don't fit fall away and the circle closes.

When I left that church and my marriage fell apart, only one person reached out to me. Only one person seemed to even notice I had gone. I have fallen away and am still falling somewhere, while the tight orbit of that church continues.

11

THE VIOLENCE OF OUR FAITH

PALY NEVER FELT AFRAID IN AMERICA UNTIL DONALD Trump was elected president. Paly is Muslim and lives in Cedar Rapids, which is home to the oldest standing purpose-built mosque in America. I met Paly when our girls became friends in preschool. My daughter and hers immediately hit it off in their classroom of two-year-olds because they were the most verbal. The girls were in the same classroom from two until they were four. By the last year that our girls were in class together, the presidential campaign was ramping up and the daily drive to school included sound bites from candidates on NPR. By that time Donald Trump was calling Mexicans rapists and murderers, and my daughter was asking questions. "Does this man hate all brown people?" she asked. "Even my friend?"

The next year, my son was in the same class as Paly's twin girls. I would see her at pick-up and drop-off and we'd shake our heads in silent sympathy over the news. There were other parents wearing MAGA hats and dressing their kids as Donald Trump for Halloween, so we didn't talk too openly, just sympathetic looks and "Can you believe this nonsense?" sighs. The day after the election, we hugged each other. We both had been crying in our cars.

Paly is from England. She and her husband, Haroon, moved to Cedar Rapids after living briefly in Boston. While driving through town, Paly and Haroon followed signs for the Mother Mosque and were surprised to learn that Cedar Rapids is the home of the oldest standing mosque in the United States. In Boston, they hadn't attended services often. Haroon went to prayers, but Paly, with her small children, rarely went. In Cedar Rapids, she felt drawn to the community because here in the prairie it was nice to be around people who looked like her and shared her faith.

It's not that her Christian neighbors and friends have ever treated her poorly, she insisted, it's just a relief to be in a place where she doesn't feel like she has something to prove. Paly notes that she presents as a "normal white mom." She has a British accent, but besides that, she notes that people are often surprised to learn she's Muslim. That's exactly what she wants. She wants people to get to know her first and then get to know her religion. "It makes them rethink their prejudice," she tells me. Not that she thinks people are prejudiced, just that they don't understand what it really means to be a Muslim.

She and I meet in a noisy coffee shop. The shop has only been open a few months, but Paly already knows half the people in the room. She was active in the community and was on the parent advisory board of the preschool. She tells me she never really felt separate from the community here until the election. Seeing people she knows, people her husband works with, posting such hateful things on Facebook about Muslims in America and supporting that man, that man who is now the president—well, that really gave her pause. "These are the people I've had in my home. The people I've fed, and then I see them posting on Facebook like I am the enemy, like I am the problem."

She never felt afraid going to the mosque either until after the election. There was one day, when there was a Trump rally being held just down the street from the mosque. Trump supporters would be gathering just as Sunday school at the mosque would be ending. For the first time since moving to America, Paly was afraid. She wasn't the only one. City police stood watch near the mosque, just for protection. Paly says the police have been kind and understanding. "The mosque has been here for forever, Muslims have been in Cedar Rapids forever, we are neighbors and business owners, the police know that even if our neighbors sometimes forget," she tells me.

I tell her how segregated Sunday is. How so many people in town don't even know about the mosque. She says there is something to that. She knows that's why she started going to services, why she sends her girls to Sunday school—because in this majority white and Christian town, they can be near people like them, so they can learn about their faith. It's not that she wants to keep them isolated, it's just that they are the diversity and sometimes that wears on you.

There is a comfort in being somewhere where you have nothing to prove.

I ask her if she might not even notice how it affects her, living in a majority Christian place. She replies that if she didn't notice before, she notices now. It's in the news—the unveiled racism of the White House. People debating and justifying why immigrants like her and her husband are the problem. If she had peace before, she doesn't have it now.

Paly is part of a group of Muslim and Jewish women who meet regularly to find ways to combat prejudice in their communities. They began meeting right after the 2016 election and have organized community outreach efforts. Paly tells me about a conversation she had with a Jewish woman and about what they would do if it got worse in America. Paly tells me the woman looked at her and said, "Worse? America is as bad as I've ever seen it."

* * *

Faith in America is under attack. On June 17, 2015, Dylan Roof entered the Emanuel African Methodist Episcopal Church in Charleston, North Carolina, and shot and killed nine black people. On February 22, 2017, in Olathe, Kansas, Adam W. Purinton fatally shot Srinivas Kuchibhotla. Purinton walked into a bar where Kuchibhotla was having an after-work beer with his friend. Purinton thought they were Muslim and screamed at the men to go back to where they came from before open firing. On Saturday, October 27, 2018, a man burst into a synagogue in Pittsburgh, Pennsylvania. He shouted "All Jews must die!" and opened fired. Eleven people died. Six more were hospitalized. In 2017, antisemitic violence increased in by 57 percent.[1] Violence against Muslims has increased since 2015, correlating with the rise in anti-Muslim rhetoric perpetuated by Donald Trump's administration.[2]

America is a nation of Christians. Seventy percent of people in America identify as Christian.[3] Our policies and cities and schools are built around having Sundays off for church, Wednesday nights off for church. We celebrate Christian holidays with time off from work and school. Our Congress is 91 percent Christian. We've never had a Jewish or Muslim president. Having a Catholic president in John F. Kennedy was wild enough. Our pledge of allegiance and our money declare that we are "one nation under God."

Christianity is so much a part of our culture and politics that it's hard to understand the one without the other. And as such, America demands that those of different faiths, or no faith, wrap and twist their lives around our values and beliefs—our holidays, our music, our political outlooks. Assimilate we tell them, or go home. No matter if this is their home. No matter if they were here before us. When we say be like us, when we say fit in, what we mean is be white and be Christian.

This is another story of faith in Middle America. The story of those whose faith is shoved to the edges. Whose religion is stigmatized and met with violence. While church buildings are crumbling, left to neglect and nostalgia, there are actual people dying because their religion isn't viewed as appropriate. Because it isn't deemed American enough. It's the story of people who live in the shadows. Who try to pass. Who do their best to be good, to break down walls and barriers, who day after day still carry the burden of racism and hate in their bodies.

During the 2016 presidential campaign, I sat in a church in Cedar Rapids and listened to a pastor preach that if Christians didn't vote for the godly candidate, Christians in America would be persecuted for their beliefs. He said this to a horrified audience of over 500, upper-middle-class white people. That whole year on Facebook, I watched as friends and former pastors shared stories about the oppression white Christians face in America. Of course, they didn't say "white" but they meant it. I know they meant it because when Dylan Roof shot nine people in a black church in North Carolina no one said a word. And Kuchibhotla, who had lived in our town and worked at the engineering company here, who knew my husband and his friends—when he died, not because of his actual faith, but because he looked like he could be Muslim, no one said a word. Not in that church anyway. Not in many churches.

Two days after the attack in Pittsburgh, one of my former pastors shared a story on Facebook, which alleged that ESPN edited out references to Jesus in a story about football player Tim Tebow.[4] "There has never been a worse time to be a Christian," declared my former pastor. This pastor's feed is filled with dire warnings about how Christians in America are going to be banned, soon, if we are not vigilant. His appeals, which ignore, the attack on Muslims and Jews, are part of a larger trend in faith in America. Tisa Wenger, professor of religious history at Yale University, identifies this trend in her book *Religious Freedom: The Contested History of an American Ideal*, when she writes that throughout American history "the most frequent and visible articulations of American religious freedom were exclusive, even coercive. The dominant voices in the culture linked racial whiteness, Protestant Christianity, and American national identity not only to freedom in general but often to this freedom in particular."[5] A white Christian pastor, ignoring the violence against Muslims while perpetuating a victim narrative for Tim Tebow, is part of the story of faith, most notably the stories we fail to tell. And these silences are inextricably linked to race, power, and class.

It shouldn't be shocking that in the face of such religious violence in America, a religious leader would choose to focus on a white man, who is not being censored in the slightest. Rebecca Solnit in her essay "Whose Story (and Country) Is This?" writes, "In the aftermath of the 2016 election, we were told that we needed to be nicer to the white working class, which reaffirmed the message that whiteness and the working class were the same thing and made the vast nonwhite working class invisible or inconsequential. We were told that Trump voters were the salt of the earth and the authentic sufferers, even though poorer people tended to vote for the other candidate. We were told that we had to be understanding of their choice to vote for a man who threatened to harm almost everyone who was not a white Christian man, because their feelings preempt everyone else's survival."[6]

The stories we tell center white Christian men. Popular books and literature that feature young boys and men as the main characters are marketed to all. Stories featuring girls and women are sidelined, even more so if those women are women of color. When I was nine, I asked a pastor why the Bible always talked about men and mankind. "'Men,'" he said, "means all people." Years later, during an argument about faith, Dave said the same thing to me. "Mankind in the Bible refers to all people!" Changing that was, in his view, politically correct nonsense.

It's a position that, whether semantically correct or not, reveals the level of entitlement over a narrative of who is seen and who is unseen. In the stories of faith I grew up with, men were allowed a full range of emotion: King David, who calls on God to destroy his enemies. Absalom rising up against his father the king. Jonah stewing under his tree, looking out on the city God saved but he hates. Job crying out to God for his miserable fate.

But the rage of good women in the Bible is all in the subtext. Nowhere is there an Eve angry for being removed from Eden and the loss of her two sons. Where is Esther, where is her horror and pain watching the genocide of her people? Or Ruth, who followed her miserable mother-in-law to a foreign land and had to listen to that lady bitching as if she felt nothing?

The women allowed to have feelings in the Bible are always the villains. Michal sneering at David that he ought to put his clothes on and stop dancing like a naked fool. She is indicted for her words, but hadn't she just been married, abandoned, and then taken back by this man? Used as a political pawn, then ignored for Bathsheba. Then there is Sarah, who beat her maidservant Hagar, blaming her for what should have rightly fallen on the shoulders of Abraham. And Job's wife, who Biblical scholars condemn for telling her husband to curse God and die. But wasn't she just wishing him a swift end to the suffering that they had walked through hand in hand?

These narratives of our faith spin out into our culture so that the imagination and bodies of marginalized people are forced to exist in a vast land that refuses to make room for them. And white Christians believe that they are entitled to this space, this land, these politics, this faith, this story—any loss, any oversight, is an offense worthy of reprisal. These stories and their narrative hegemony teach us too that men who express anger are good or, at worst, just misunderstood, and women who bend and serve and repress are doing what they are supposed to do.

Paly giving food to people who insult her. Seeing her try to pass as Christian in order to assure her neighbors, is another story of faith in Middle America. One not privileged, one rarely told. And it makes a difference whose story is told. Because when we ignore the stories of others, when white people frame ourselves as the victim in a narrative of oppression that we created, we fail to see the true humanity of others.

The immigration debate has deeply divided America. And that divide has been made deeper and wider by the Trump administration's attempt to end illegal immigration and immigration from Muslim countries. But who gets the empathy in this debate is a matter of narrative perspective. In a poll conducted in the spring of 2018, 68 percent of evangelicals said that America has no responsibility to house immigrants.[7] In response to the argument that Jesus was a refugee in Egypt as a child, and therefore Christians ought to be welcoming of immigrants, Paula White, a prominent evangelical minister who is close to the president, noted that Jesus wasn't breaking the law but the immigrants in our country are.[8]

The theology behind that argument is spurious, but it exists in the hearts and minds of Christians in America and it affects policy. It affects how we treat others. Shortly after taking office, the president put into effect his travel ban against majority-Muslim nations. The ban was immediately challenged as religious discrimination but was upheld in a narrow Supreme Court ruling.[9] On November 25, 2018, border patrol agents gassed women and children on the border between Mexico and the United States.[10]

Of course, many religious leaders have fought back against the travel ban and are condemning the actions on the border, but Christianity is a faith divided. And the actions of one set of Christians don't cancel the actions of the other. And the darkness and cruelty of faith in America is just as much a part of the story as the kindness and goodness. For every church like the Asian American Reformed Church of Bigelow, there are others who resist immigration. For every city like Minneapolis, which has the largest urban population of Hmong, due in large part to the efforts of faith-based nonprofits, there are so many others rejecting and vilifying Muslims in the name of Christianity. But the truth is more likely that we live in a place that does both. A place where we dine at the houses of our neighbors, but post cruelties about them on Facebook. Where we will give the shirt off of our back for someone in need, and then vote against them at the ballot box.

I don't have an answer for the dissonance, it's as deep and real and painful as any part of American history. And it's tempting to look away from it, to instead focus on the positive. Look at all the good that is done. But this violence is still part of the story of faith and religion. And if we want to know what is happening with faith in America, we have to look at all the effects of faith, even the violent ones. Even if we believe that we are not that kind of Christian, not that kind of white person, not that kind of man, not that kind of woman. Even if we don't believe we are racist and we say we love our fellow man, if we have sat in a church that was silent to suffering, we are complicit. If we have turned the other way when children were being tear gassed, that violence is now our religion. And we have to grapple with that, we have to hold it in our hands, so we never forget.

12

RECLAIMING OUR FAITH

I CAME TO THE CONFERENCE LATE AND TIRED. I had planned to be on time, but my life had just fallen apart.

I'd asked for a divorce in September after coming home from a work trip and discovering some of my Halloween decorations missing. Dave found them offensive—pictures of witches and a sign that read "Drink Up, Witches," which had made me laugh in a stupidly delighted way. The way some people laugh at YouTube videos of men throwing ping-pong balls, I'm a sucker for a witch pun.

We all have those moments of breaking. A dear friend of mine told me she knew her marriage was over when her then husband woke up, surveyed the breakfast she'd made of French toast, sausage, and omelets with feta cheese, and declared, "You know I hate feta!" Another told me hers was over when her husband went out and got chicken wings with friends hours after she'd delivered their first child.

Mine had broken the moment I came home and saw my witch decorations gone. There were of course many small schisms leading up to that moment, ones that had gotten so big we didn't know how to reach across anymore. But scanning the hutch cluttered with pumpkin drawings and vintage Pyrex was the first moment I felt lost in the depths of our divide.

How had we gotten here? I wonder this often about my marriage, and about America. The only answer I have is that we refused to see the truth of the other in the beginning. We'd spun narratives around each other—adding and deleting, until what we had no longer represented a truth, but instead was the story we wanted to tell.

As is the way with the ends of things, this one took a while. I didn't move out until December. And then there was Christmas and the New Year, which happened in moments. Swaddling my screaming infant nephew and watching him settle, sigh, and sleep in my arms. Cold Chinese food and podcasts while assembling furniture. Crying to Netflix shows while I tied careful bows onto my children's Christmas presents. My own son screaming with laughter while I tickled him, his head rearing back and smashing into my face, giving me a black eye that made me look like I felt inside. Waking up on a deflated air mattress next to the squirming bodies of my two children, feeling both devastated and completely content.

Now it was January and there was this conference, Mystic Soul, that my friend, the talented writer and author Deborah Jian Lee, had told me to go to. The conference was designed to center the voices of people of color at the "intersections of mysticism, activism, and healing." The conference took place in Chicago, a city I'd skirted around on my travels but hadn't stopped in. People who live in rural Illinois insist that Chicago isn't part of who they are. Several had encouraged me not to report from the city at all, arguing that Chicago wasn't even Midwestern.

During the 2016 election, more than half of Hillary Clinton's 2.9 million Illinois votes came from Chicago's Cook County. Yet, Donald Trump won 91 of the state's 102 counties.[1] Demographically, Illinois is over 70 percent white, but Chicago itself is only 45 percent white.[2] I hear talk like this all the time. People in Cedar Rapids say that Iowa City isn't really part of the Midwest because of the professors and students at the University of Iowa. Michelle, a pastor in St. Louis, says people in Missouri say it all the time about her city too. But what they mean, she tells me in a conspiratorial tone, what they always mean is, "that's where the black people are."

In the introduction of Frances Fitzgerald's comprehensive history of Evangelicalism in America, she explains that her book, titled *The Evangelicals*, is specifically about white Evangelicals. She notes that the book "purposely omits the history of African American churches because theirs is a different story, mainly one of resistance to slavery and segregation, but also of the creation of centers for self-help and community in a hostile world."[3] It's a compelling explanation and a comprehensive book. And yet, it is titled *The Evangelicals*. If a book is written about the black Evangelical church, it will have to be called *The Black Evangelicals*, won't it? Further segregating and marginalizing a story of faith so central to American history. It deserves more than just a paragraph of mention.

It's a racist narrative trick we always do when we talk about Christianity in America. When we say "Christian" we mean white people. When we talk about great Evangelists in American history, we mean Billy Graham, not Martin Luther King. King is a black activist. But Graham is allowed to be for all. This is the narrative trick being pulled when people tell me to disregard Chicago. It's the erasure of othering. As if centuries of struggling together and against one another hasn't left us all deeply and irrevocably changed.

Chicago's story, like the story of St. Louis, Minneapolis, and Iowa City, is a Midwestern story. The story of the black Evangelical church is the story of the Evangelical church. These stories might not fit the narrative we want to tell about ourselves, but they are as essential to the meaning of who we are as any other story. So, I went to Mystic Soul and showed up late. Sneaking into a lecture, where everyone gathered was immediately asked to stand up and find someone who looked completely opposite from them and begin a conversation. So many people look different than me. I stand up and get to work.

* * *

Mystic Soul is part of a growing movement among people of color to decolonize their faith from an understanding of Christianity that erases them. Lee explains in her article about Mystic Soul, "For some, that means decolonizing their Christian faith from white patriarchy and capitalism. For others, that means connecting to ancestral faith practices, such as Yoruba, Buddhism, ancestor veneration or particular tribal traditions. For others, it's an amalgam, a synthesis of severed history, personal heritage and truths from other traditions. For most, it means imagining a spiritual wholeness that has been denied for so long, and chasing it with abandon."[4]

Decolonizing Christianity means that this conference has been rethought from the placement of the chairs to the music and the lights. At every Christian conference I've attended, rows of chairs face a stage with a single podium. The music is played by a band and is more often performed rather than participatory. Sessions involve sitting and listening to experts, with little interaction or discussion. In contrast, at Mystic Soul the chairs in the conference hall are placed in a circle, and beautiful lights hang from the ceiling. The sessions include yoga, Kintsugi, live podcast tapings, and dance classes focused on liberating the body. The music is led a cappella. People clap and stomp, using their whole flesh as instruments of worship.

Prayers are poems.

In the words of Amina Ross, an artist who leads the session on decolonizing the language of black and white, "Decolonizing often means just having fun."

Teresa Pasquale Mateus, a trauma therapist and author of *Sacred Wounds: A Path to Healing from Spiritual Trauma*, is one of the founders of the conference. In her article, Lee recounts how Pasquale Mateus turned to mysticism to heal from sexual trauma and from there came back to Christianity. But Christianity as practiced in America didn't have room for her. "The movement's white leadership, white theological framework and expensive retreats largely excluded people of color and their concerns, says Pasquale Mateus. 'It still didn't speak to the wholeness of me,' she says, particularly 'my brownness.'"[5]

From this dissonance, Mystic Soul was born. The traditions practiced here are nothing new—it's a type of contemplative Christianity. But what is new is the focus on activism and reconnecting contemplative Christianity to its roots in communities of color. Lee, who is Chinese American, wrote that going to Mystic Soul was a kind of group therapy for her. A safe space to practice her faith in a community of people who do not seek to erase her.

I came to the conference as a reporter—someone seeking to understand the faith story of Christianity in the heartland. But I am also a white middle-class woman. Fifty-three percent of us voted for Donald Trump. During the first lecture, the speaker asked us to think about who our ancestors are, who do we honor with our lives and our faith? Immediately, I thought of my grand-mother in purple polyester, chain-smoking in my aunt's trailer in Oklahoma and bitching about my mom. I had to stifle a laugh. This was who I was sup-posed to honor? A long line of women who sat around, drank tea, and com-plained? How was I supposed to enter this space with that history following me? Pondering that question, I understood that my whole life I had felt alien-ated and confined by the language of more conservative Christianity without even thinking how my faith, my body, and my history might alienate others.

I put my recorder down and I listen.

* * *

Robyn Henderson Espinoza identifies as a gender-queer Latinx. Henderson Espinoza is a PhD in philosophy and ethics, and when they stand near the lectern in Hamming Hall, the energy they emit is so real and alive in a way I have a hard time articulating.

Henderson Espinoza wears dress slacks and a bow tie. Their shirt sleeves rolled up. They talk about how as an academic, for so long, they lived a life of the mind. "We elevate the mind over the body," explains Henderson Espinoza, "and we sure as hell don't know what to do with the heart." Their journey required learning their own story rather than the story of others, and in the process they connected with themselves and their spirituality.

My whole life, I've been taught that to be a better practitioner of my faith I must read the Bible and a myriad of other books. I must sit and pray, listening for disembodied signs and signals that come from outside of me. I've spent two years driving around America, looking for answers to what is happening to faith in America in the land, life, and stories of others. Henderson Espinoza is instead saying that connection to spirituality comes from within.

This feels like a joke—the call was coming from inside the house.

But it also alarms me. If the answer is reconnecting to who we are and our presence in the world, if it's a fleshy faith of my sinew, my bone, and my flesh, then I am fucked. I've been trying for so long to become a master of my body that I have no idea what it even is anymore.

The very next day, I attend a workshop titled "Liberating the Body." Led by artist and yoga instructor Stacy Patrice, it's not something I would ever usually sign up for—not before this weekend anyway and what does it even have to do with my line of inquiry? I wonder. But I am here, and I want to throw myself into this space as much as I can. I want to honor its intentions and the work of the people around me. And the one thing I notice is how ill-fitting I am in this skin of mine. How tired I feel. How I'm still bruised from the black eye my son gave me over Christmas. How my back aches from the air mattress. How my fingers hurt from assembling furniture. And the uncanny knowledge of what my face represents to the people around me.

To be clear, I am an American woman. I have always been aware of my body. I have always been painfully aware of how it fits or doesn't fit in spaces. I read articles on clothing it, washing it, feeding it. I joke with my friends that every American woman should be awarded a PhD in nutrition by the time she reaches eighteen. But because I've never felt at ease in my body, I've been taught to be more than it. To have, like Henderson Espinoza articulated, a life of the mind, eschewing the heart and the skin that made me too much of a woman, too much of a liability. So my whole life I've had a hard time inhabiting my body. Because to fully occupy my body means to come to terms with desires and feelings that Christianity has told me are sinful. It involves listening and validating urges to eat, to rest, to make love. In order to temper those bodily needs, I've whittled my flesh down to bones and muscle, grateful for its compliance and nothing more.

At the beginning of the workshop, Stacy Patrice has us close our eyes and sing. We sing one note, starting deep and low, then going higher and higher. Already I'm struggling with this. We are supposed to find our level. The one we want to sing out at. All I can come up with is midrange.

The next part of the workshop involves moving our bodies. We stomp and jump. We shout and spin. I keep my eyes closed so I can focus on myself. I try to listen to the sound of the music and nothing else, not to the quiet voices in me telling me I have no rhythm, telling me I look like a fool. But they take over, and at one point I open my eyes and stop, frustrated. Patrice shouts out that we are created by the divine. Our bodies are divinely inspired, therefore using them, and connecting with them is part of worship—holding back is selfish.

I'm struck by her words.

For so many years, I've been going to white churches where no one claps. No one moves. Sometimes I do—slapping my thighs and singing out. But usually I'm an anomaly. My then husband would always give me a look that suggested I settle down, and so would others around me. Sometimes I'd offer an excuse—I grew up in Baptist churches in Texas. The admission would bring tight smiles. This lack of movement is a staple of many nondenominational Evangelical churches in the Midwest. It's a move of dignity and sobriety, of comportment, of communicating the value of control and restraint. The last time I'd attended church with my husband, the verse for the sermon was the anthem of this belief system, 1 Peter 5:8: "Be sober, be vigilant; because your adversary the devil, as a roaring lion, walks about, seeking whom he may devour." My husband had patted my hand as the verse had been read, and I had instinctively slapped it down.

But in this workshop, I hear Patrice's words and wonder if Christians who insist that flesh is sinful have got it all wrong. If we believe our bodies are God-made, then binding them, restricting them, forcing them into molds that we struggle against, that's not scripture, that's repression. Faith in America as it exists and how it is practiced in the heartland is more about control than it is about freedom.

I stomp my feet and yell—twirling, shrieking, gyrating, worshipping. I don't feel foolish because I am not alone. I am just another free body moving in a sacred space.

* * *

That night I went out with friends. I needed a reason to celebrate. My birthday had come and gone without much fanfare. So had Christmas. So had New Year's. My friends in Chicago organized a night out for me, and after liberating my body I went and drank whiskey and ate a pizza so thick it could have been a casserole.

The night before he died, Jesus broke bread and told his friends it was his body. He drank wine and told them it was his blood. This symbolism lives on in the Christian faith—it is Eucharist, eating and drinking in the spirit of thanksgiving.

In *Baptized, We Live*, a Lutheran pamphlet by Daniel Erlander, he writes that being Lutheran is "seeing crucified Jesus as God in flesh, God entering the darkness of our existence to gather us into a kingdom of wholeness, unity, and peace. Seeing God in all creation but specifically in the water of Baptism and the bread and wine of Eucharist."[6]

That night, with my friends—Catholics, Jews, Protestants, and atheists—in the frigid darkness of a Chicago January, we ate and drank in the spirit of thanksgiving. We were celebrating my divorce. My survival through the holidays. It seems callous to celebrate the end of a marriage, but that's what we did. And it seemed that God was in that meal too—hidden in the ordinary whiskey and pizza. Bread and wine. Body and blood. Something had been broken. Something had died this year. My marriage. My faith. My understanding of what it was to be a person of faith in America. Or maybe it had always been dead, now I was just seeing it.

Once, while I was lamenting the loss of politically neutral space in the wake of the 2016 election, a friend kindly told me that for people who are queer, or trans, or people of color, no space has ever been politically neutral. I was just privileged enough to not see it for a while. The point, he said, was not to beat myself up about this, but ask myself what I was going to do. America's broken divide. America's complicated Christianity. These deep wounds I've been probing have always been bleeding.

When I first interviewed her for this book, the woman who would become my pastor, Pastor Ritva, told me "If churches are dying in America, let them die. If faith is dying in America, let it. After all, we believe in resurrection. There can't be new life without death." Americans abhor death, we gloss over it. We are one of the few countries that practice embalming, so death looks like eternal life. Even our idioms eschew death. *Look on the bright side. Think positive. Everything happens for a reason.* We cannot just sit with death.

During the Holy Week of Easter, Holy Saturday is the day most churches do not celebrate. We move from Good Friday to Easter Sunday, failing to sit with that day in between. The day that Christ lay dead in a tomb—undergoing the Harrowing of Hell. But it's just as necessary as any of the other days. Whether Holy Week is celebrated literally or symbolically, the day of death's fullness is necessary to the celebration of resurrection.

So many of the dissertations and books I've read about revitalizing the American church fetishize the new life, without fully grappling with the death. They are full of tricks and tips to disrupt our old tired concepts of church and to breathe new life in them. Drums. Incorporating video. Community groups. Flannel shirts. Tattooed pastors. Church in a bar. Church on a bus, in the train, in the rain, church with a beer.

All of them fine ideas, but all of them missing the point entirely. They fetishize growth and size over true and lasting change. Creating a corporation out of a church, a factory out of a faith.

In the Eastern tradition, Holy Saturday is celebrated with a midnight vigil, during which all the candles are extinguished and the congregation waits in darkness and silence for the declaration of the resurrection. And if I believe anything about the Christian tradition, it's that if unity is to be achieved we must sit in that silence, dwell in that darkness, waiting.

* * *

On the last day of the Mystic Soul conference, I took a class with the artist and activist Amina Ross. Ross leads workshops to help people decolonize their language. That day, the word we focused on was "darkness." Darkness in Christianity has come to symbolize the bad things—sin, a world without God. But using darkness as a metaphor has damaged our imaginations, Ross told the room, which was filled with people of color, all with skins of varying hues of darkness. If we only see darkness as negativity, then it will limit our imaginations.

Ross read from Adrienne Maree Brown's *Emergent Strategy*, a passage I found relevant and disturbing:

> We are in an imagination battle. Trayvon Martin and Mike Brown and Renisha McBride and so many others are dead because, in some white imagination they were dangerous. And that imagination is so respected that those who kill, based on an imagined, racialized fear of Black people, are rarely held accountable.
>
> Imagination has people thinking they can go from being poor to a millionaire as part of a shared American dream. Imagination turns Brown bombers into terrorists and white bombers into mentally ill victims. Imagination gives us border, gives us superiority, gives us race as an indicator of capability. I often feel I am trapped inside someone else's imagination, and I must engage my own imagination in order to break free.[7]

With those words, Ross challenged us to rethink our concept of darkness—leading us in free movement, free association, and free writing on the topic of what is darkness. One woman told our group that darkness to her was her womb—it was life. Another person said darkness was rest—sleep. Still another said darkness was the mystery of the ocean.

I thought of central Idaho, where 1,416 square miles near the Sawtooth Mountains are designated one of America's few dark sky reserves. The challenging isolation of the land there means that it has resisted development and electrification. Darkness is preserved and cherished by residents, who follow lighting ordinances and work to eliminate light pollution in order to honor the darkness of nature. This is what I think about as Ross guides us through these exercises. I think of the sky. I think of darkness worth preserving and worth seeing. Darkness that is cherished.

I also remember my friend Kristin holding me as I cried. Cried for my losses. Cried for my children. Cried for everything that belief had cost me. I told her I wanted to be through this part, these dark days. Kristin had lost her son just days before his first birthday. I had gone to stay with her then. Holding her as she cried. And now, here we were again, four years later, roles changed.

"You can't skip these parts," she told me. "You cannot erase them. You will never get over them. What you learn is to live with them. Honor them—they are part of you now."

At the end of the conference, I think again about my ancestors—those problematic white women. They would hate me, I think. They would hate my divorce. They would hate my writing. They would hate my religion and the way I dress. But I wonder if that's because maybe in me they see another way of living—a liberated future. Maybe in me they see their wrongs. But if that's the truth, I still carry the consequences of their actions with me and in me.

The story of Mystic Faith is not a story for me to colonize. But it is still part of my story, I am just on the other side. Those women on porches were not just passive. Their ability to sit and fan required the subjugation of others. They benefited from a racist culture and an exclusionary faith. And in turn, I too have participated and benefitted. My silences have been oppression. By participating in worship that through its very makeup and omissions silences and brutalizes others, I've joined in white supremacy. There are no excuses good enough. The only question is, what am I going to do about it?

13

THE FIRE OUTSIDE

O N THE NIGHT OF HOLY SATURDAY, I STAND with a huddle of congregants near the front door of the church. The lights are dim and we all hold unlit candles. My two children are eagerly pressing themselves to the front of the crowd. When Pastor Ritva asks everyone to move in closer, my daughter says loudly, "I'm close enough, thank you!" And everyone laughs.

Outside the church is a holy fire.

It's March 31 and there is snow outside. The wind is brutal. The fire is barely alive. The pastor goes outside and lights a candle from the blaze, which is contained in a rusting fire pit. I am disappointed a little. I wanted my first religious ritual flame in a beautiful container—an Olympic torch, perhaps? I don't know what I wanted it to look like, just that I wanted the container of holy fire to be more beautiful.

Sheltering the weak flame with her hands, the pastor hustles inside and we begin to pass the flame. Lighting candles in turn—children, adults. My four-year-old son whispers, "Dis seems dangerwous!" We all laugh.

But it is dangerous. Fire is dangerous. Love is dangerous. Hope is dangerous. Belief and faith are dangerous. And I am here tonight with my children because of danger. Because of burning and searching and the charred ruin of a fire inside.

One month before Easter, I met with Pastor Ritva and she asked me if I wanted to become a member of her church. I began going to St. Stephen's six months ago, right after I decided to end my marriage. I had wanted to go to the church for years because so many of my friends go there. I've dragged my family to church picnics on the lawn and pool parties at the local park. In the past few years, I'd gone to evening services and helped pack lunches for school children on Wednesday nights, sometimes bringing my kids, other times going alone. But we'd always stopped short of attending Sunday services. The reason was because my husband refused to sit through a sermon given by a woman. He also thought gay pastors were heresy. St. Stephen's has both and a large rainbow flag hanging in the hallway.

Unrepentant heretics.

I tried for so many years to go to other churches with him. I tried so hard to bend my heart to fit the limits of other orthodoxies. I tried until I hurt so much, that I had to say "no more." I had to say, "This is what I need." And in speaking my needs, I ended our marriage.

I started going to St. Stephen's after I asked for a divorce and just showing up was all I could muster most weeks. Everything in me was broken. Being who you are shouldn't ruin everything. Asking for what you need shouldn't blow up your life. It shouldn't cost you your love and your home.

But it did.

During this time, I was obsessively watching a TV show called *Santa Clarita Diet*, where Drew Barrymore plays one half of a husband and wife realtor team who accidentally turns into a flesh-eating zombie. Her husband, played by Timothy Olyphant, reacts to her human-eating habit with love and support. I know it is a fictional television show, but I would find myself on Saturday nights watching, laughing, and eventually crying. It wasn't fair that Drew Barrymore could be loved and supported while she ate people, but being a Lutheran broke up my marriage.

And now, Pastor Ritva wanted to give me the chance to be a member— to officially become a Lutheran. I wanted to. I didn't want to. I was tired of belonging to places that didn't seem to want me. Too often, belonging meant being controlled rather than being free. Too often, belonging meant giving up instead of becoming. Also, becoming a member would make real the divide. I could no longer pretend I was just hanging out in the back of this small church on Sundays. I would be part of the congregation. I'd have a name tag waiting for me in the hall.

I explained this to Pastor Ritva over coffee. Earnestly trying to tell her how afraid I was. Afraid that once I was in, they wouldn't like me anymore.

"I'm not good at believing the things I'm supposed to," I said. "I'm not good at being the person I'm supposed to be."

Pastor Ritva nodded, "Me either."

I'm trying to talk her out of this. I tell her my doubts about hell. I tell her how previous pastors have chided me for my writing. I tell her that I will write about this church and does she want that? Does she really want that? The bemused smile never leaves her face. She listens without interrupting. When I stop talking, she simply says, "of course." And I am out of objections. Because when it's all said and done, I want to belong too. So I agree.

She tells me we will do the membership service on Holy Saturday, the day that Jesus lay in the tomb. It's a day that dwells on death and only death. It's a liturgy of darkness. Between Good Friday and Easter Sunday, Holy Saturday is the day between dying and resurrection. It's a day of death. A day of dwelling in that divide. I don't want to dwell in a divide. I want resurrection and I want it now.

* * *

Everyone has plans for a faith revival. Craft beer at church, or what about some smartphone apps? More retreats, more Bible studies, which are now called "doing life together groups," outdoor concerts, and picnics. Let's re-invent it! Let's disrupt it! Let's cut away rite and ritual until all we have are guitars and lights. Put this church in a restored warehouse, sell coffee, start programs for children—all good changes, all superficial. At some point it feels like putting makeup on a corpse. A kind of *Weekend at Bernie's* of faith.

I see this in other places in America too—something is broken in America. Something is dead. We see that, but instead of probing the complexities of the problem, we want to immediately perform CPR. We want to skip dwelling on the death to get right to the fix—the resurrection.

Media outlets hire conservative voices to bridge the "liberal media" divide without even fully understanding what that divide is or what it means. Politicians push to pass legislation to fix our problems with taxes, fix our problems with immigration, but meanwhile we are out here dying by our own hands. Hammers pulled out to pound in nails, without even understanding what's broken. We don't like to sit with a corpse.

Holy Saturday forces us to sit with a corpse. For a day, we have to sit and look at death and ponder what it means. On this Holy Saturday, it's windy and cold. I take my daughter to a class for kids of divorce in the morning, and when I drop her off I feel impoverished. I feel that way I used to feel when in college I had no money for food and I didn't know how to ask for help. I wanted so much to be able to be okay, for everything to be okay, to be able to do this on my own, that I couldn't admit that for months I lived off of Doritos. So I'd lie or make jokes, "This is a new diet!" I'd tell my friends. And they'd laugh and move on.

But here in this brokenness and loss, I cannot pretend. I cannot laugh and move on. I have two witnesses with me. They force me daily to confront this end—all ends. We talk about their grandfather who died before they were born. The brother of one of their friends who died before he was one. We talk about how mommy and daddy's marriage died too. They want answers and certainty and I can't give it to them. All I can give are my assurances that things will be okay, better even, if not now then soon. Soon.

But bless them, they probe the darkness, with "Why" and "Why" until I feel excoriated, my insides a cold, empty fridge.

When I pick up my daughter from the class, she is happy. She shows me a picture of a unicorn she drew. She tells me the lessons she learned. She asks for another class. I'm surprised and happy. She didn't want to be told it was okay. She didn't want new life, she just wanted someone to sit with her and let her know she wasn't alone in this loss.

I wonder at what age we learn to stop looking at death. At what age do we learn to shun darkness? Isn't it better to elbow into it—examine it, touch it, feel its edges?

After a cold Easter egg hunt, my kids and I get dressed go to church. There we observe the fire outside and watch Pastor Ritva bring it inside.

* * *

Over coffee, just two weeks before Holy Saturday, Pastor Ritva gives me a pamphlet about what it means to be a Lutheran. I am going to become a member of the St. Stephen's congregation and she wants me to be prepared. I went to a Lutheran college and once wrote a satire of the 95 Theses about my college for the student newspaper and duct-taped it to the chapel doors. I feel like I know a lot about what it means to be a Lutheran. Faith is about believing the unbelievable.

At this point, I don't know if I believe the Bible as a book of historical fact or a work of literature. Metaphor is often more powerful than the limits of the literal, so for now I enter the metaphor. That we have to enter these parts of death, we have to go in gladly and willingly. Otherwise there can be no resurrection.

At our meeting, Pastor Ritva reminds me of a story of Jesus. In the book of John, right after Jesus's triumphal entry into Jerusalem, there is a story about two Greek men who want to see Jesus. The disciples tell Jesus, and he responds by saying, "The hour is come, that the Son of man should be glorified. Verily, verily, I say unto you, Except a corn of wheat fall into the ground and die, it abideth alone: but if it die, it bringeth forth much fruit.

He that loveth his life shall lose it; and he that hateth his life in this world shall keep it unto life eternal."

Two men came to look for Jesus and he told them about death. Put a seed into the ground and let it die. Only then can it grow.

Seeds outside of soil are inert things. Put into the ground, a seed falls apart—it becomes a fluid nourishment to the seedling. It's a dissolution. A rearrangement of the elements. Seeds swell with water. Roots push their way out, anchoring first into the ground, then the plant unfurls upward. And at some point in all of this, the seed ceases to be a seed and becomes something else.

This is why I still have a faith. This is why I haven't given up entirely. That moment of passing from one form into the next is mysterious and almost magical. Because when I see death in faith, it is not an end, it's a rearrangement of elements. What is inside is released and allowed to reach upward.

When two men come looking for Jesus, he tells them about death.

In the past three years, I have been looking for faith in this land. I've been trying to understand what is changing, what is passing away, what remains, and what we hold onto. What I found was a death: crumbling churches by forgotten roads, declining attendance, hallways of abandoned organs, younger generations moving away, farm crisis, and land lost.

I've also experienced my own loss—first the loss of a church, then the loss of my marriage. In losing them, I've lost my narrative consistency, the entire concept of who I thought I was supposed to be. In this way, it's no different than the way the communities I've been in feel about the closure of their own churches. Who are they now that the mainstay of their community is gone? Who and what is driving this narrative if it's not bookended by worship? So much of love and faith is about aspiration—what do you reach for when it is gone?

I've been told not to dwell on these losses. People I interview are adamant that I talk about growth, the new and exciting things that are happening—and there are new things, new churches, new movements—but they all seem just like iterations of what is being lost. And besides, I want to enter into this place, where whatever came before is disintegrating and turning into something else.

A friend who is a farmer scoffs at the seed metaphor. "It's not really death. The seed is just doing its job. Death is putrid and it means a complete end," he tells me. It comforts me that he doesn't see nature's cycles as death.

When a tree falls, when a field goes fallow, it's not death, it's a cycle of regeneration. "You just have to look at the bigger picture," he tells me.

"In that case, does anything ever really die?" I ask. He is not a Christian, he only believes in nature. So I ask if our bodies die and become part of the earth if that's really a death.

"Just the consciousness," he says. "Our bodies return to what we were meant to be—good earth."

* * *

When something is dying, often it's better just to guide its passage. As people of faith, we don't believe that death is an end. Death just means we return to what we are meant to be.

Faith in America is dying. Populations are changing. Churches are closing. Small towns and schools consolidating. It seems callous to say we are turning into what we were meant to be. It seems like one of those platitudes, like, "everything happens for a reason."

The forces of faith, economics, politics, immigration, the internet, technology, racism, and homophobia can be so devastatingly felt. But it's also wrong to say that this is the end. Maybe the answer is to just sit with death, to hold it in our hands, to examine it, watch it, and realize that it's not death at all.

My daughter shows me the handout from her divorce class. It has a section for parents that instructs us to allow our children to feel whatever they need to feel—anger, rage, depression, hope, relief, sadness, and despair— whenever they need to feel it. There is a story in the handout about a little girl who keeps everything bottled up and then hits her little brother and carries the advice that it's okay to feel what you need to feel, but it's not okay to hurt other people in the process. It's such a cliché to find meaning in a children's lesson. But I do.

I think of people who have voted out of fear. Who have altered the landscape of America with angry reactionary responses to the forces of change in their own lives. In 2016, 75 percent of Trump voters were angry at the way government was operating, compared to 18 percent of Clinton voters. [1]A CNN poll in December 2017 showed Americans are still angry—68 percent saying they are angry with the direction the country is headed. [2]

I see it in the farmer who voted for Trump despite the fact that he had his best years under Barack Obama. I see it in the pastor's wife who told me that city values are sinful. I see it in the women who volunteer in their churches, but are silenced in the decision-making process. I see it in the people of color tired of fighting and having no one listen. I see it in gay Christians, so tired of being in a space that most often would rather not have them. We are all tired. We are all angry.

We are all a voice clamoring to be heard.

The anger is a fire outside that has been brought inside. I dip my candle in it and then pass the light on. We walk into the church, light in hand, and sit in the pews in the dark, the only light is the light we hold.

Fire is a chemical reaction between air and fuel. It's destructive in its path, but when controlled it gives us heat.

In "Barn Burning" by William Faulkner, Ab Snopes is a poor white sharecropper who burns the barns of rich landowners. Through the eyes of Flem, Snopes's son, Faulkner observes that "the element of fire spoke to some deep mainspring of his father's being, as the element of steel or of powder spoke to other men, as the one weapon for the preservation of integrity, else breath were not worth the breathing, and hence to be regarded with respect and used with discretion."[3]

Fire preserves and fire destroys. So does anger.

* * *

On Holy Saturday, I sit with my children in church. They are antsy and crawl all over the pews and whine, asking when church will be over. But I make them sit with me. I make them pause in this space. And when I go up to the front of the church to publicly acknowledge I'm a Lutheran now, they come with me. My four-year-old waves an "Alleluia" banner so enthusiastically he smacks me in the face. I stand there with my friend Mel and I follow Pastor Ritva's lead—renouncing the devil, affirming my commitment to the church.

A year ago, I was sure I'd never be a member of another church. I was never going to commit to a faith community again. I was through with the pain and the control. But after going to this place for months and seeing their daily effort to make the world around them a better place—their programs to feed kids at the local schools, donate to homeless shelters, march in the Pride parade, and partner with the mosque—I had hope.

I told Pastor Ritva I didn't know what I believed. And she said she was okay with that. I said maybe there wasn't a hell, and she said she didn't think so either. I told her I didn't want to work in the nursery and she said they didn't have one—kids are welcome in the service. Later, when my husband emailed her telling her I was violating God's will, she stood by me. Where other pastors had told me my writing was heretical, Pastor Mark, the associate pastor of the church, shared my words on the church's Facebook page.

People often ask me why I believe still. I ask myself that too. Why do I still go to church through all of this? Why do any of us? If faith is changing and dying, why do we still participate? Why do 70 percent of Americans still profess to be Christian? Even more still believe in God.

I imagine it's the same reason why people in Middle America don't just move. In these small towns, where loss has eviscerated them and their communities, they stay. Because this place is part of their identity—this land that gives and destroys, that creates and breaks.

I still believe in mystery and reverence. I believe in something beyond myself that I cannot know, although I don't know what that is. And that unknowing is what I believe faith to be. I believe in church because whatever else, it's an intentional community of people trying to do good in a world that could use more of it. I believe in it because it's part of me. I go to church because it's the one time in my week where I, with my friends, sit and acknowledge mystery. I stay in Middle America because it's human nature to want to live near the things you love, even if they are ghosts.

Before I stood to commit myself again to a human endeavor so messy and so fraught, we blew out the candles and released the "alleluias." Our church has a tradition of hiding the "alleluias" during the period of Lent. On the Sunday before Ash Wednesday, we collect flags with "alleluia" written on them and put them in a box. For those six weeks, no songs are sung with alleluia. But now our candles are extinguished. We've sat with the fire. We've held it. We honored it and extinguished it.

But now the "alleluias" are released. My kids eagerly clutch the banners that have been passed out to replace our candles. When I walk up to the front, both of my children have banners in their hands. So I stand in the church, blinking back tears, while my children wave their "alleluia."

This isn't an end, nor is it a beginning. We will be back here next year. Putting away alleluia, sitting with death, holding the fire from outside in our hands. It will mean something different the next time and the next.

I am comforted by the ritual of liturgy, the way it provides a scaffolding to access the mystery of what is happening around us. The cycles will continue. Seeds will break down into plants. Plants will grow to produce a seed. Death. Life. Resurrection.

The next morning is Easter, and I stay up too late fussing over the baskets. I'd wanted to have a party. I'd wanted to celebrate. But I was also very tired, and I couldn't muster up the wherewithal to plan such a thing. So it's just us. We go to church, then we come home. On this, the day of resurrection, the day of life, I collapse in exhaustion. I spend the day lying on the couch watching TV with the kids, letting them eat all the candy they want. Later, we eat dinner as a picnic in front of the TV, laughing and clinking our cups like we are fancy. It occurs to me, we have had the best party, one far more compassionate and full of grace and naps than anything I would have planned.

It occurs to me that I am here again, ready again, to live my life according to my beliefs. To walk again in a dangerous speculation. And I can think of nothing more American than that—to keep trying to find something better, and if it fails you, you make it. You wrest it from the earth. In an act of both life and death.

NOTES

Introduction

1. Andrew R. L. Cayton, "The Anti-Region," in *The American Midwest: Essays on Regional History*, ed. Andrew R. L. Cayton and Susan E. Gray (Bloomington: Indiana University Press, 2001), 148.
2. Phil Christman, "On Being Midwestern: The Burden of Normality," *The Hedgehog Review* (Fall 2017), https://iasc-culture.org/THR/THR_article_2017_Fall_Christman.php#endnotes.
3. Christman, "On Being Midwestern."

1. Dangerous Speculation

1. Louisa May Alcott, *Transcendental Wild Oats* (Carlisle, MA: Applewood, 2011), 56.
2. http://www.thearda.com/rcms2010/r/s/19/rcms2010_19_state_name_2000_ON.asp.
3. http://cara.georgetown.edu/caraservices/requestedchurchstats.html.
4. "Empty Pews: Stats Show Sharp Religious Decline in Iowa," *Des Moines Register*, October 25, 2015, https://www.desmoinesregister.com/story/life/2015/10/25/empty-pews-stats-show-sharp-religious-decline-since-1970s/74468978/.
5. Jennifer Sherman, *Those Who Work, Those Who Don't: Poverty, Morality, and Family in Rural America* (Minneapolis: University of Minnesota Press, 2009).

2. The Heart of the Heartland

1. http://uipress.lib.uiowa.edu/bdi/DetailsPage.aspx?id=396.
2. Roger Finke and Rodney Stark, *The Churching of America, 1776–2005: Winners and Losers in Our Religious Economy* (New York: Rutgers University Press, 2005).
3. Finke and Stark, *The Churching of America*, 79.
4. O. E. Rolvaag, *Giants in the Earth* (New York: Harper, 1999), 489.
5. https://news.gallup.com/poll/11146/women-clergy-perception-reality.aspx.
6. https://www.census.gov/newsroom/releases/archives/2010_census/cb11-cn192.html.
7. https://news.gallup.com/video/175130/trend-line-church-attendance-today-similar-1940s.aspx.
8. https://religionnews.com/2014/12/11/1940s-america-wasnt-religious-think-rise-fall-american-religion/.
9. Frances Fitzgerald, *The Evangelicals* (New York: Simon and Schuster, 2017), 86.
10. Fitzgerald, *The Evangelicals*, 197.
11. https://www.prri.org/research/american-religious-landscape-christian-religiously-unaffiliated/.

12. http://www.businessinsider.com/state-domestic-migration-map-2016-to-2017-2018-1.

13. Bethany Moreton, *To Serve God and Wal-Mart: The Making of Christian Free Enterprise* (Cambridge, MA: Harvard University Press, 2009).

3. Yearning for Better Days

1. http://www.hrsa.gov/healthit/images/mchb_child_mortality_pub.pdf.

2. http://dph.illinois.gov/sites/default/files/publications/publicationsdoil-opioid-data -report.pdf.

3. Val Farmer, *The Rural Stress Survival Guide* (Brookings: South Dakota State University, Cooperative Extension Service, US Dept. of Agriculture, 1994), 15.

4. Barney Wells, Ron Klassen, and Martin Giese, *Leading Through Change: Shepherding the Town and Country Church in a New Era* (Bloomington, MN: Churchsmart Resources, 2005).

5. David L. Brown and Kai A Schiff, *Rural People and Communities in the Twenty-First Century* (Cambridge, MA: Polity, 2017), 109.

6. https://www.acf.hhs.gov/sites/default/files/opre/nis4_report_congress_full_pdf _jan2010.pdf.

7. https://www.ruralhealthinfo.org/topics/violence-and-abuse#prevalence.

8. Jennifer Sherman, *Those Who Work, Those Who Don't: Poverty, Morality, and Family in Rural America* (Minneapolis: University of Minnesota Press, 2009), 105.

9. https://www.npr.org/2016/10/23/498890836/poll-white-evangelicals-have-warmed-to -politicians-who-commit-immoral-acts.

10. https://www.npr.org/2016/10/23/498890836/poll-white-evangelicals-have-warmed-to -politicians-who-commit-immoral-acts.

11. https://www.washingtonpost.com/news/acts-of-faith/wp/2016/11/09/exit-polls -show-white-evangelicals-voted-overwhelmingly-for-donald-trump/.

12. https://www.prri.org/wp-content/uploads/2016/10/PRRI-2016-American-Values -Survey.pdf.

13. Milan Kundera, *Ignorance* (New York: Harper, 2003), 5.

14. William Andrews, *Antiquities and Curiosities of the Church* (London: W. Andrews and Co., 1897), 294.

15. Robert Blair, *The Grave: A Poem* (London: W. P. Hazard, 1851), 3.

4. The Pew and the Pulpit

1. Andrew Miles and Rae Jean Proeschold-Bell, "Are Rural Clergy Worse Off? An Examination of Occupational Conditions and Pastoral Experiences in a Sample of United Methodist Clergy," *Sociology of Religion: A Quarterly Review* 73, no. 1 (2012): 23–45.

2. https://www.insidehighered.com/news/2016/04/27/study-finds-those-graduate -education-are-far-more-liberal-peers.

3. Milan Kundera, *Immortality* (New York: Harper, 1999), 258.

4. http://www.pewforum.org/fact-sheet/changing-attitudes-on-gay-marriage/.

5. http://www.pewresearch.org/fact-tank/2017/04/26/among-white-evangelicals-regular -churchgoers-are-the-most-supportive-of-trump/.

6. Lynn Garrett, "Critics and Activists Add Ferment to Religion Publishing," *Publisher's Weekly*, March 23, 2018, https://www.publishersweekly.com/pw/by-topic/industry-news/religion/article/76402-a-left-turn-for-religous-publishers.html.

5. The Church of the Air

1. https://www.barna.com/research/americans-think-women-power/.
2. http://www.pewforum.org/religious-landscape-study/gender-composition/women/.
3. https://www.barna.com/research/americans-think-women-power/.
4. https://www.fcc.gov/reports-research/reports/broadband-progress-reports/2016-broadband-progress-report.
5. https://www.cjr.org/special_report/midterms-2018-iowa-rural-broadband.php/.

6. Room at the Table

1. Deborah Jian Lee, *Rescuing Jesus: How People of Color, Women, and Queer Christians Are Reclaiming Evangelicalism* (Boston: Beacon, 2016), 125.
2. http://www.pewforum.org/religious-landscape-study/region/midwest/.
3. https://www.nytimes.com/2016/11/22/upshot/the-states-that-college-graduates-are-most-likely-to-leave.html.
4. https://www.prri.org/research/survey-anxiety-nostalgia-and-mistrust-findings-from-the-2015-american-values-survey/.
5. https://www.usnews.com/news/politics/articles/2017-10-24/despite-diverse-demographics-most-politicians-are-still-white-men; http://www.pewresearch.org/fact-tank/2016/07/01/racial-gender-wage-gaps-persist-in-u-s-despite-some-progress/.

7. A Muscular Jesus

1. https://www.christianpost.com/news/john-piper-god-gave-christianity-a-masculine-feel-68385/.
2. https://www.desmoinesregister.com/story/opinion/columnists/2014/05/05/argument-against-kinnick-stadiums-pink-locker-room/8718293/.
3. https://today.duke.edu/2015/12/chavesstudy.
4. https://www.christianitytoday.com/women-leaders/2015/october/state-of-female-pastors.html.

8. The Asian American Reformed Church of Bigelow, Minnesota

1. http://www.city-data.com/city/Bigelow-Minnesota.html.
2. https://www.nytimes.com/1964/08/02/archives/11-a-m-sunday-is-our-most-segregated-hour-in-the-light-of-the.html.
3. https://www.huffingtonpost.com/scott-thumma-phd/racial-diversity-increasing-in-us-congregations_b_2944470.html.

4. Oscar Wilde, *The Soul of Man under Socialism* (ValdeBooks, 2009), 2.
5. http://sacsis.org.za/site/article/271.19.

9. Bridging the Divide

1. https://www.census.gov/geo/reference/ua/uafaq.html.

10. A Den of Thieves

1. https://www.christianitytoday.com/news/2017/september/how-many-churches-in
-america-us-nones-nondenominational.html.
2. https://abcnews.go.com/US/story?id=93111&page=1.
3. https://www.christianitytoday.com/edstetzer/2018/february/reflections-on-mega
-church.html.
4. https://www.christianitytoday.com/karl-vaters/2016/march/dear-andy-stanley-please
-be-small-churchs-ally-not-our-enem.html.
5. Lyle E. Schaller, "Megachurch!," *Christianity Today* 34 (1990): 34.
6. http://people.duke.edu/~dee4/articles/eagle_hist_megachurch.pdf.
7. David D. Eagle, "Historicizing the Megachurch," *Journal of Social History*, advance
access, February 25, 2015, 4
8. Eagle, "Historicizing the Megachurch," 5.
9. https://www.washingtonpost.com/news/made-by-history/wp/2018/02/22/billy
-graham-americas-pastor/.
10. http://content.time.com/time/world/article/0,8599,1653276,00.html.
11. https://www.huffingtonpost.com/2012/08/20/megachurch-high-may-explain
-success_n_1813334.html.
12. https://www.motherjones.com/crime-justice/2018/08/the-churchtoo-movement-just
-scored-a-historic-victory-for-victims-of-sexual-abuse-willowcreek-community-church
-bill-hybels/.

11. The Violence of Our Faith

1. https://psmag.com/social-justice/anti-semitic-incidents-in-the-us-rose-57-percent
-in-2017.
2. https://www.citylab.com/equity/2018/03/anti-muslim-hate-crime-map/555134/.
3. http://www.pewforum.org/religious-landscape-study/.
4. https://www.getreligion.org/getreligion/2018/10/9/espncom-trims-j-word-out-of
-big-florida-rite-in-tim-tebows-life?fbclid=IwAR2Yyr5XD73hQkIadzQMe_q8pl1J4Alv
_cUXnZjTzXQ5kbOoD4WFuyNOgVo.
5. Tisa Wenger, *Religious Freedom: The Contested History of An American Ideal*
(Chapel Hill: University of North Carolina Press, 2017), 1.
6. https://lithub.com/rebecca-solnit-the-myth-of-real-america-just-wont-go-away/.
7. https://www.vox.com/identities/2018/11/20/18097319/white-evangelicals-immigration
-trump-honduras-caravan-theology.

8. https://www.vox.com/2018/7/11/17561950/trump-evangelical-ally-jesus-immigration-law.

9. https://www.usatoday.com/story/news/politics/2018/06/26/supreme-court-upholds-president-trump-immigration-travel-ban/701110002/.

10. https://www.nbcnews.com/news/world/san-diego-border-crossing-shut-down-after-migrants-try-entering-n939891.

12. Reclaiming Our Faith

1. http://www.chicagotribune.com/news/data/ct-illinois-election-urban-rural-divide-2016-htmlstory.html.

2. https://www.census.gov/2010census/data/.

3. Francis Fitzgerald, *The Evangelicals* (New York: Simon and Schuster), 10.

4. http://religiondispatches.org/christians-of-color-are-rejecting-colonial-christianity-and-reclaiming-ancestral-spiritualities/.

5. http://religiondispatches.org/christians-of-color-are-rejecting-colonial-christianity-and-reclaiming-ancestral-spiritualities/.

6. Daniel Erlander, *Baptized We Live* (St. Paul, MN: Augsburg Fortress Press, 1981), 10.

7. Adrienne Maree Brown, *Emergent Strategy* (Chico, CA: AK Press), 22.

13. The Fire Outside

1. https://www.usnews.com/news/the-report/articles/2018-02-23/angry-voters-got-trump-elected-now-anger-may-help-democrats.

2. https://www.usnews.com/news/the-report/articles/2018-02-23/angry-voters-got-trump-elected-now-anger-may-help-democrats.

3. William Faulkner, "Barn Burning," in *Selected Short Stories of William Faulkner* (New York: The Modern Library, 1993), 8.

LYZ LENZ has been published in the *New York Times*, *BuzzFeed*, the *Washington Post*, *The Guardian*, *ESPN*, *Marie Claire*, *Mashable*, *Salon*, and others. Her book *Belabored: Tales of Myth, Medicine, and Motherhood* is forthcoming from Norton. She also has an essay in the anthology *Not That Bad: Dispatches from Rape Culture* edited by Roxane Gay. Lenz holds an MFA in creative writing from Lesley University and is a contributing writer to the *Columbia Journalism Review*.